At No Time

SEAGULL
BOOKS
•
CELEBRATING
40 YEARS

THE GERMAN LIST

ILSE AICHINGER

At No Time

SCENES AND DIALOGUES

TRANSLATED BY STEPH MORRIS

LONDON NEW YORK CALCUTTA

This publication was supported by a grant from the Austrian Federal Ministry for Education, Arts and Culture, and the Goethe-Institut India.

Seagull Books, 2023

First published in German as *Zu keiner Stunde* by Ilse Aichinger
© S. Fischer Verlag GmbH, Frankfurt am Main, 1957

First published in English translation by Seagull Books, 2023
English translation © Steph Morris, 2023

ISBN   978 1 8030 9 144 0

British Library Cataloguing-in-Publication Data
A catalogue record for this book is available from the British Library

Typeset by Seagull Books, Calcutta, India
Printed and bound by WordsWorth India, New Delhi, India

CONTENTS

1

French Embassy

POLICEMAN OUTSIDE THE FRENCH EMBASSY. Walking the dogs again?

HOUSEMAID FROM THE ACROSS THE ROAD. I am.

POLICEMAN. Nice day today!

MAID. Isn't it!

POLICEMAN. Or is it?

MAID. It is—a very nice day.

POLICEMAN. The mistress' greyhounds really look their best, under the blue sky.

MAID. For sure.

POLICEMAN. Their lovely white coats!

MAID. Come here, Josiah!

POLICEMAN. Josiah?

MAID. A made-up name.

POLICEMAN. What about the other one?

MAID. Rosethorn.

POLICEMAN. Josiah and Rosethorn.

MAID. Both made up.

POLICEMAN. Quite right too.

MAID. Yes.

POLICEMAN. Well, what a fine day it is!

MAID. The mistress has gone out. Committees.

POLICEMAN. And the master?

MAID. At work. It's the kids I feel sorry for. Stuck in school all day.

POLICEMAN. I don't.

MAID. The city is so quiet today, as if there was no one in it.

POLICEMAN. That would be no bad thing.

MAID. As if we were all alone.

POLICEMAN. Does it bother you?

MAID. This time of year—

POLICEMAN. Not a cloud in the sky.

MAID. Soon be ice-skating time for the kids.

POLICEMAN. As if the morning were standing still!

MAID. It isn't.

POLICEMAN. Well the prophets could never have dreamt they'd be carved in stone on church columns mid-speech.

MAID. Come here, Josiah!

POLICEMAN. Where are you off to?

MAID. The littlest master has a new tricycle. He's riding in the park, round the fountain.

POLICEMAN. I see.

MAID. I'm picking him up.

POLICEMAN. I'd save my energy for something better.

MAID. Can't think what.

POLICEMAN. I can.

MAID. I don't doubt it.

POLICEMAN. The prophets—

MAID. Can leave me be!

POLICEMAN. I wanted to say something else.

MAID. What?

POLICEMAN. You and I—

MAID. Nothing else?

POLICEMAN. The blue sky—

MAID. Come here, Rosethorn!

POLICEMAN. This day, the dogs, this corner by the embassy—

MAID. Oh dear.

POLICEMAN. The doves!

MAID. What about them?

POLICEMAN. Marie!

MAID. And what are you talking about?

POLICEMAN. The stonemason from the church was in my dream last night.

MAID. Other people's dreams—

POLICEMAN. There was a space free, on the last column, left-hand side!

MAID (*uneasy*). I have to fetch the little one. The mistress—

POLICEMAN. And when I saw you this morning crossing the road, Marie, I had the idea you and me and the dogs—

MAID. We're leaving now!

POLICEMAN. With the embassy in the background. We'd fit in nicely, Marie!

MAID. That's not my name!

POLICEMAN. It would help the stonemason out. Us too! The last free space. The clear sky!

MAID. No, thank you.

POLICEMAN. No more afternoons, Marie, no evenings, no nights. Just the morning, always just-past eleven, and you and me. The dogs—

MAID (*horrified*). Josiah, Rosethorn!

POLICEMAN. It would be a lovely morning to stay in!

MAID. No morning is that lovely.

POLICEMAN. The sun!

MAID (*looks at the sky*). The wind is building up.

POLICEMAN. It'll bring snow. It'll be cold out walking with the little boy, who isn't even yours.

MAID. That's as may be.

POLICEMAN. One word, Marie, and no more—

Maid shakes her head.

POLICEMAN. We'll be together for ever! The word!

MAID (*staring firmly at the sky*). I can see clouds coming.

POLICEMAN. Before they reach us!

MAID (*to the freezing dogs*). Let's go.

POLICEMAN. Marie!

MAID. I don't want to be on a column.

LITTLE BOY IN THE PARK. Your hands are cold, Marie!

MAID. It'll be ice-skating time soon.

The Prophet Elijah rides through the sky above them in a red chariot.

2

At No Time

The Student enters the attic, closes the door behind him and walks towards a crate of books behind a strut. He bends down and starts searching.

GNOME. Busy, busy?

STUDENT (*absent-minded*). Yes.

> *He notices the Gnome, wearing a tall, green hat, standing on a box and gazing with one eye out over the city through the skylight.*

STUDENT. What are you doing here?

GNOME. Nothing. I'm looking out at the city, at the green dome on the palace over there. (*Pointing to his hat.*) I'm comparing one green with another. There's no end to it. Especially with all the gardens in this district.

> *The Student, bent over his crate, doesn't respond.*

GNOME. Between three and four, without fail. It gives my day some structure. That way I feel I'm continually standing here. What about you?

STUDENT. I'm looking for some lecture notes.

GNOME. You too? Always here between three and four?

STUDENT. Whenever I need notes.

GNOME. And when do you need them?

STUDENT. When I can't find them downstairs. I'm studying ship-building.

GNOME. At what time?

STUDENT. All the time.

GNOME. At no time?

STUDENT. Always.

GNOME. Pity, otherwise we'd meet up here more often.

STUDENT. I wouldn't get very far then.

GNOME. How far do you want to get?

STUDENT. As far as I can. On a ship—

GNOME. I often see them gliding past on the river while I'm comparing the green of the meadows with my hat. I could recommend you.

STUDENT. I have to finish studying first. I'd like to get a bit further.

GNOME. I also compare the green of the horizon with my hat. I have connections there, too.

STUDENT. First I have to—

GNOME. You passed an exam today.

STUDENT. Yes. How do you know?

GNOME. As I was comparing my hat to the green of the patina spread over the roof of the Engineering Faculty, you were awarded a distinction.

STUDENT. It was the last-but-one. Only after the last exam—

GNOME. Feel free to approach me at that point.

STUDENT. I have various offers already.

GNOME. I'm happy to recommend you.

STUDENT. I'll be going back home first. To get married. And then—

GNOME. I'm always here, between three and four!

STUDENT. I have offers in Germany and America! It's just a question of—

GNOME. Always between three and four.

STUDENT. A question of—

GNOME. And I can be at your service wherever there are shades of green. They are frequently seen on ships.

STUDENT. On new ones, true.

GNOME. The sea has lots of them.

STUDENT. I won't be constructing the sea. I'll be constructing boats.

GNOME. The rivers!

STUDENT. Certainly not riverboats.

GNOME. I want to use all my connections in green to pull strings for you!

STUDENT (*gets up, brushes his hair back*). Here are my notes.

GNOME. You have no idea how many there are in the world. Not just the greens of the roofs and gardens, also the seaweed, the pondweed, the ocean floor, all distinct and nuanced—

STUDENT. I have to go now!

GNOME. I could demonstrate just using my hat and the spire on the Polish church, or that dome, or the green of the treetops around the arsenal—

STUDENT (*leaving*). Sadly—

GNOME. If you just came up to see me now and then—

STUDENT. It's my last term.

GNOME. Just between three and four—

STUDENT. Either have lectures or practicals then. And when there's time off, I have to revise for my final exam and finish drawing cross-section of a ship.

GNOME. Or on your last day, the day of your final exam! Between three and four.

STUDENT. I'll be packing my case.

GNOME. It will be a misty day, all eyes grey, domes yellow, roofs black. You will get all-round distinctions.

STUDENT. God willing!

GNOME. You will have said goodbye to your friends already.

STUDENT. Then I will make my way to the station!

GNOME. There will be an hour left, at least an hour. You will remember there is still a crate of books up here, maybe you need one or the other. You open the attic hatch. You go to the book crate, bend down and look through. No, you don't need any more books. It's all over now. You get up—

STUDENT (*impatient, the notes in his hand*). And?

GNOME. You look towards the skylight. You sigh—

STUDENT (*in the open hatch*). I won't sigh!

GNOME. I assure you! You will sigh. And then—

STUDENT. I'm off now!

GNOME. Then I will recommend you to the green of the sea.

The hatch slams.

The Gnome giggles and carries on looking through the skylight over the city.

3
Gulls

THE COMEDIAN ON THE RECORD. Eeny meeny miny mo—

FIRST GIRL. Ducks!

SECOND GIRL. It's so good! You can tell it's ducks.

THIRD GIRL. Unless it's gulls.

SECOND GIRL. Gulls!

FIRST GIRL. Seeing as you've never heard one!

SECOND GIRL. You get river gulls, seagulls—

FIRST GIRL. These are ducks.

THIRD GIRL. You've had the record a long time now.

FIRST GIRL. Mum and Dad bought it for Easter last year.

SECOND GIRL. On Good Friday.

THIRD GIRL. We were at your house at the time.

SECOND GIRL. Remember?

FIRST GIRL. Maybe they'll buy a record again this year.

SECOND GIRL. Doves!

FIRST GIRL. And again next year.

THIRD GIRL. Gulls!

SECOND GIRL. Always a comedy record featuring animals.

THIRD GIRL. When you're a hundred you'll have really good selection. Then your dad will come—your mum will be dead by then—walking down the hallway . . .

A bell rings.

EMILY (*hoarsely*). Yes? (*Opens the hallway door.*)

FATHER. I've brought you another record, Emily.

EMILY. Come in, Daddy!

FATHER. I reckon it's rather funny.

EMILY. That's sweet of you.

FATHER. The gulls you'd been missing.

EMILY. The gulls! You think of everything.

FATHER. Your two friends not here?

EMILY. No, not today. One of them died at eighty, Daddy—

FATHER. Oh yes.

EMILY. And the other at ninety.

FATHER. Of course. I forget that every year.

EMILY. Is it Good Friday today?

FATHER. I think so. There've been no church bells all day.

EMILY. Then it'll be Good Friday.

FATHER. I've never got it wrong, Emily.

EMILY. No.

FATHER. You must admit I've brought you a record on Good Friday every single year.

EMILY. Yes, Daddy.

FATHER. It's been my pleasure, every time.

EMILY. Mine too!

FATHER. And they've always been spot-on, the records!

EMILY. Always! I'm very proud of you, Daddy!

FATHER. The pleasure it brings me, right from the first time when I walked home from town, in the sun, with your mother, passing the open church doors, everyone in their robes, and the thought suddenly overwhelmed me—what are we going to take home for our little Emily?

EMILY. Then it was the ducks. Then I was twelve.

FATHER. The next year it was the doves.

EMILY (*laughs*). The doves!

FATHER. And then the chickens.

EMILY. Turkeys and guinea fowl.

FATHER. And lambs, hoopoes—

EMILY. Now, it's twenty-seven years since Mummy died.

FATHER. The year she died it was the goldfinches. She died in March, and Easter was in April.

EMILY. The goldfinches!

FATHER. That's a great record, too.

EMILY. A stand-out record.

FATHER. If you already have a large collection, and a sense of the various different cries, but I wouldn't recommend anyone start with it.

EMILY. It's incredible what the record industry has put out in just twenty-eight years!

FATHER. And I must say, we couldn't be more grateful.

EMILY. All that's missing are gulls.

FATHER. Till today, Emily, till today! (*Laughs.*)

EMILY. I've held off going to the seaside till this day for that very reason. I thought one day you'll bring me that record, too.

FATHER. You've been very patient, Emily, and your patience will be rewarded!

EMILY. You know I wasn't always patient, Daddy. Between seventy and eighty—

FATHER. That phase passed, Emily.

EMILY. Especially when I was seventy-three.

FATHER. The year I brought you the record with the cats.

EMILY. The cats, yes.

FATHER. You had heart trouble that year.

EMILY. I just about managed to hide my disappointment.

FATHER. Your disappointment?

EMILY (*emphatically*). I mean it was a wonderful record, Daddy—

FATHER. It was a most exceptional record.

EMILY. I know!

FATHER. We laughed our heads off! All that amorous mewling and caterwauling—

EMILY. But I was having my first heart problems, Daddy, and I didn't know how long a weak heart can go on. I thought, Ursula will be proved right after all, and I'll never hear gulls.

FATHER. You didn't breathe a word.

EMILY. No, and in the end, I forgot all about it anyway thanks to the catfight between the angora tom and the Siamese.

They both start laughing, again.

EMILY (*somewhat out of breath*). Even Ursula and Daisy forgot about it.

FATHER (*also out of breath*). True.

EMILY. And then in my seventy-seventh year I faced the dilemma whether to visit the seaside or not? I'd been offered a cheap trip, but I didn't take it. I trusted you, Daddy! Ursula and Daisy went that year. They had a wonderful time.

FATHER. They died soon after.

EMILY. But not me.

FATHER. You did the right thing, Emily.

EMILY. But how did you pull it off, Daddy? Just in my hundredth year, right on my hundredth birthday, which is also Good Friday—

FATHER (*barely concealing his pride*). It was easy. The young man just happened to have the record.

EMILY. He happened to have it!

FATHER. Came in yesterday.

EMILY. What did he say when you walked through the door?

FATHER. Nothing at all. I asked, 'Do you have the record with the gulls?' And he said, 'Yes.' And handed it to me.

EMILY. No matter that you'd been waiting for eighty-seven years! That Ursula and Daisy died waiting!

FATHER. No, we didn't go into all that.

EMILY (*pointing her finger*). You scamps!

FATHER. But, afterwards, I did have to sit on a bench in the park for a while turning the record over and over on my knees in the sunshine till I believed it.

EMILY. I woke today feeling especially bright. I noticed there were no bells ringing, and I knew today was Good Friday, the day my daddy brings me the funny records! I rolled to the window in my wheelchair and saw the plate-glass of the galleries opposite, sparkling. Then I was more certain.

FATHER. You had doubted me yet again!

EMILY (*archly*). On Good Fridays, I can never quite believe it is Good Friday.

FATHER. But now, Emily, now you really believe it?

EMILY. As soon as I saw you, Daddy.

FATHER. And wait till you hear the gulls!

EMILY. I can't wait to hear them!

FATHER. I'll fetch the gramophone.

EMILY. The horn is right by it.

FATHER (*from the room next door*). I know what to do, Emily.

EMILY. You never forget.

FATHER (*breathless*). A beautiful sunny day today!

Emily has fallen asleep.

The rusty crank of the gramophone turns in the next room.

FATHER. And now!

The needle scratches on the record.

FATHER. And now, Emily!

THE GULLS ON THE RECORD. Crucify him! Crucify him! You must crucify him. Crucify him! You must—

FATHER. That can't be the gulls.

He puts the needle down in a different place.

THE GULLS. —him. You must crucify him, crucify—

FATHER. I'd like to hear the ending!

He puts the needle down at the end of the side. Giggles, which also resemble the wind on the sea.

FATHER. This bit's funny, Emily, can you hear? This bit's funny! It's the gulls, Emily!

Emily is no longer breathing.

4

The Fleeting Guest

The Poem, dressed as a young man, knocks on a door.

GIRL (*opening the door*). Good evening!

POEM. How are you doing? I'm glad you could see me.

GIRL (*lively*). Oh, me too! I almost wasn't up to it, but now—

POEM. Now?

GIRL. I've written a decent poem! Just before you came. I was lying on my bed, staring at the ceiling. The room was full of smoke and I was watching the sparrows outside the window but not hearing them. It was cold in here, the way rooms can be in spring—

POEM. I know.

GIRL. I counted the creases in my counterpane, lacking the strength even to add to them. From the kitchen I heard the clatter of cutlery. A meal was being prepared, but not for me.

POEM. Yes.

GIRL. I was hungry, but couldn't rouse myself. Because I wasn't suffering, I felt incapable of suffering. All pain was elsewhere. In the dentist's surgeries, on the sinking ships—there it raged, but not in me.

POEM (*sympathetically*).You poor thing.

GIRL. A child might have fallen over in the park and grazed his knee all bloody. So distant from me. A thief might have been caught at a jewellers'—

Poem nods.

GIRL. So distant from me. And even the girls buying rings with their own money, who had—if not pain—at least a goal, something you might term 'tonight'—

POEM. Didn't you think I might come?

GIRL. No, I knew nothing. And to be honest, it would have changed none of that.

POEM. Of course not.

GIRL. Because the day was running through my fingers like an un-prayed rosary.

POEM. That's a fine simile.

GIRL. For without pain there is no solace, and I was honest enough not to invent the former for the sake of the latter, (*hastily*) as I held no hope of salvaging this day, jammed in the reel like a worn, tattered typewriter ribbon, and just lay there—

POEM. I'm just wondering how you were able to—

GIRL. If the poem hadn't come, I wouldn't have got up and opened the window. I wouldn't have put on coffee, smoothed the coun-terpane or let you in!

POEM (*disappointed*). So it's only thanks to him that I'm here.

GIRL.Yes, and that tonight we can still go out together! To Meierei, to the park, or—

POEM. I'm afraid I'll have to disappoint you.

GIRL. Disappoint?

POEM. I wasn't planning to stick around. I simply wanted to return the grammar book you lent me.

GIRL. And tonight?

POEM. Tonight I have to lie on my bed and wait for someone who isn't actually looking for me. (*He unmasks himself and vanishes.*)

GIRL (*rushing to the open window*). Stay!

The cries of the sparrows can be heard.

5

In the Voice of the Old Lady

A Strange Child approaches a Child who is returning home from the park with her Mother.

STRANGE CHILD. Why aren't you having a party?

CHILD. A party?

MOTHER. Because I'm not keen on parties.

STRANGE CHILD. But why?

MOTHER. I went to the wool shop. The ball of red wool was being unspooled for all to see, and I asked the old lady if we could buy it to decorate our room.

STRANGE CHILD. She said no?

Mother nods.

CHILD (*sadly*). She said no.

STRANGE CHILD. Why?

CHILD (*in the voice of the old lady*). When I sold the brown one, they hung wires. Since then the dancers' voices fail to reach me.

MOTHER. That's it!

CHILD. Their charming voices in the coffee break. When I sold the blue one—

STRANGE CHILD. Enough!

CHILD. They laid snares. Since then the birds fly straight past, up in the sky, in scattered flocks!

STRANGE CHILD (*puts her hands in front of her eyes*). Enough!

CHILD. You get the idea. (*In the voice of the old lady.*) The green one, frayed on the hard poplar branches; the brown one, in tatters; the blue one, flung—

STRANGE CHILD. Can no one sort this out?

Silence.

MOTHER. We prefer to pace up and down the hallway—

CHILD. Clip, clop!

MOTHER. Our faces nice and quiet.

CHILD. Quiet, yes.

MOTHER. With the noonday ahead of us.

All three stand still for a moment.

STRANGE CHILD (*serious*). There are red clouds rolling across the sky above the pilots' signatures; shells lying in the sand.

MOTHER. But we're not having a party.

STRANGE CHILD (*walking again*). I know a rental centre.

MOTHER. Too far.

CHILD. We would mourn the lions.

STRANGE CHILD. Ten black speers you can easily wind the sun and moon onto!

Mother shakes her head, scowls.

STRANGE CHILD. Beyond them the bursting fountain, and beyond that—

CHILD. Don't tempt us!

STRANGE CHILD. The second Sunday of the month, at six in the morning—

CHILD (*thoughtful*). At six in the morning?

STRANGE CHILD. Well before the folks in white shoes arrive.

MOTHER. Leave us in peace!

The Strange Child looks them both and smiles.

The Child puts one foot forward.

STRANGE CHILD. The air so clear you could slice it!

MOTHER. Quiet now!

STRANGE CHILD. Why won't you have a party?

CHILD. It's not just because of the lions. It's also the flowers, they close their petals at night.

MOTHER. Go away! I'm telling you, leave us—

STRANGE CHILD. In peace!

She vanishes.

6
Belvedere

HEAD ZOOKEEPER AT VIENNA ZOO. Good morning!

DIRECTOR OF THE UPPER AND LOWER BELVEDERE GALLERIES. And a very good morning to you, too. I believe I have briefly had the pleasure?

ZOOKEEPER. Indeed you have. I do have an appointment.

GALLERY DIRECTOR. And what brings you here?

ZOOKEEPER. I'm here about the bulls.

GALLERY DIRECTOR (*pondering*). The bulls?

ZOOKEEPER. Yes. The subject was first discussed several years ago.

GALLERY DIRECTOR. Bulls . . . Bulls . . .

ZOOKEEPER. The white Egyptian cattle, if you recall . . .

GALLERY DIRECTOR. Bulls?

ZOOKEEPER. With red eyes!

GALLERY DIRECTOR. A painting?

ZOOKEEPER. No. Bulls.

GALLERY DIRECTOR. I'm getting a glimmer of something here—but for the life of me I can't put my finger on it.

ZOOKEEPER. The idea was that they would be housed here.

GALLERY DIRECTOR. Here?

ZOOKEEPER. Yes.

GALLERY DIRECTOR. Here? (*Gestures towards the half-open window with a view up the sloping French gardens.*)

ZOOKEEPER. Between the Lower and Upper Palaces, correct.

GALLERY DIRECTOR. How many are we talking?

ZOOKEEPER. The whole herd, three hundred or so.

GALLERY DIRECTOR. That must have been before my time.

ZOOKEEPER. Before my time, certainly, but at the beginning of yours. My predecessor negotiated with you.

The Gallery Director shakes his head.

ZOOKEEPER. The zoo was too small even then. And now the herd has grown.

GALLERY DIRECTOR. I really have no recollection of this I'm afraid.

ZOOKEEPER (*vehemently*). The plan fell through at the time because it was impossible to drive the herd through the monastery gardens adjoining to the left, and the owners of the gardens to the right, all then private, also refused permission. These gardens have now become public property.

GALLERY DIRECTOR. Just recently.

ZOOKEEPER. Exactly, and the council will do everything in its power to support the zoo.

GALLERY DIRECTOR. I don't doubt it.

ZOOKEEPER. The herd can be driven through the gardens without doing much damage of course. There is no shortage of experienced drivers.

GALLERY DIRECTOR. And here?

ZOOKEEPER. Here they will be standing nose to tail. But you would still have room, even now!

GALLERY DIRECTOR. But—

ZOOKEEPER. If you opt to drain the water out of some of the flatstone ponds—all of them really . . .

GALLERY DIRECTOR. All of them?

ZOOKEEPER. And herd the animals into them. I don't think the edges would be too steep for them.

GALLERY DIRECTOR. I have no idea how agile White Egyptian Cattle are.

ZOOKEEPER. They're surprisingly nimble. And also very peaceful.

GALLERY DIRECTOR. I see.

ZOOKEEPER. And no need to worry about your view! You will still enjoy a fabulous vista through this window. Your eyes will sweep over the white crowns and white horns as if over morning mist or shimmering water—depending on the time of day. You won't miss a thing. Not for a moment!

GALLERY DIRECTOR. And what if I wish to see gravel and lawns?

ZOOKEEPER. You won't, not once you can gaze at the white herd.

GALLERY DIRECTOR. In any case, it's not just a question of my wishes.

ZOOKEEPER. Clearly it will be your responsibility to keep the herd clean and white.

GALLERY DIRECTOR. My responsibility is to the gallery visitors.

ZOOKEEPER. As long as the herd stays white—

GALLERY DIRECTOR. Irrespective of whether the herd remains black or white—what, I should like to know, are people to do who wish to saunter from the gallery of paintings in the Upper Palace to the sculptures in the Lower, who require the calm of a Sunday morning, the sound of gravel underfoot, as they switch from one to the other.

ZOOKEEPER. They should go via the street.

GALLERY DIRECTOR. It's a detour. And as I just said—

ZOOKEEPER. The question is irrelevant in any case. The lower palace will no longer house the sculptures.

GALLERY DIRECTOR. No longer house the sculptures?

ZOOKEEPER. Well, only till the first rains, till the first damp winds, till it's time to bring the herd inside.

GALLERY DIRECTOR. Bring them inside?

ZOOKEEPER. If you want to ensure their coats remain white, it's your best bet. You'll need to give orders, at the first sign of rain, as soon as particular cloud formations appear in fact, that—

GALLERY DIRECTOR. But the sculptures!

ZOOKEEPER. As you surely know, the sculpture galleries are located in the former stables. Almost everything now known as the 'Lower Palace'—

GALLERY DIRECTOR. Not my rooms.

ZOOKEEPER. Your rooms will remain unchanged. Your peace and quiet must be preserved. For the animals' sake alone. It's important they feel at peace. And their calm should be reciprocated, from these two windows at least. And if the sculpture galleries don't prove sufficient there is always the Upper Palace. Should the herd breed here under your care—

GALLERY DIRECTOR. That's what this is really about, I knew it!

ZOOKEEPER. It's about your best interests and your visitors'. It would only be in an emergency.

GALLERY DIRECTOR. Which will undoubtedly occur. As far as I can see this 'emergency' is part of the plan. What else would the cattle do here except breed?

ZOOKEEPER. Paw at the ground, stamp, shine in these optimal surroundings!

GALLERY DIRECTOR. To the best of my limited knowledge—

ZOOKEEPER. Trust me!

GALLERY DIRECTOR (*emphatically*). They will not stop at that.

ZOOKEEPER. These are white bulls. And when the sun shines—

GALLERY DIRECTOR. They won't stop when the sun shines, at the first sign of rain, or when particular cloud formations appear!

ZOOKEEPER. They have red eyes.

GALLERY DIRECTOR. What difference will that make? And in such close quarters.

ZOOKEEPER. We shall see.

GALLERY DIRECTOR. I will see, not you.

ZOOKEEPER. I'm quite sure—

GALLERY DIRECTOR. And who will feed the animals?

ZOOKEEPER. Initially the zoo will provide some of the care, along with the council.

GALLERY DIRECTOR. And the residents of the surrounding buildings who rented these apartments solely because they have views of the gardens?

ZOOKEEPER. As soon as they set eyes on the white herd they will realize what they've been missing till now. What—for years, who knows?—has made the gardens seem so empty, the morning birdsong so mocking, the gravel paths so drab. At the gentle movements of the herd they will realize what has eluded them so long, notice which way the wind blows again.

GALLERY DIRECTOR. The smell of manure—

ZOOKEEPER. Will also play a role.

GALLERY DIRECTOR. Who will clear it away?

ZOOKEEPER. As I said, initially the zoo will continue assisting with the animals' care. And after that you needn't worry about it. Once the cowherds and drivers are living in the surrounding streets, the manure can easily—

GALLERY DIRECTOR. The cowherds and drivers?

ZOOKEEPER. Appointed by yourself, naturally.

GALLERY DIRECTOR. By me?

ZOOKEEPER. Insofar as the inhabitants of the surrounding streets are willing and able to take over these duties they could remain here, obviously.

GALLERY DIRECTOR. That will be an immense comfort to them.

ZOOKEEPER. Quite. While you, of course, would be in charge of overall—

GALLERY DIRECTOR. I thought as much.

ZOOKEEPER. You are a familiar face. Your efforts on behalf of the galleries' treasures are acclaimed. If instead you simply switch your efforts to the herd—

GALLERY DIRECTOR. Instead?

ZOOKEEPER. People will soon come to accept it. Not just accept it. Soon they will hold the white bulls—

GALLERY DIRECTOR. And cows.

ZOOKEEPER. —hold the whole herd in the same estimation previously reserved for the sculptures and paintings in the galleries, for those Sunday mornings with a beguiling play of sunshine and shadows. Visitors will soon be comparing the curves and gradations of the horns and admiring the calves in the empty galleries.

GALLERY DIRECTOR. I'm still unclear why all this can't take place at the zoo.

ZOOKEEPER. For all the reasons I've just stated. Plus one more!

GALLERY DIRECTOR. The gallery would be more than happy to donate proceeds from the sale of one or two valuable sculptures towards the extension costs of—

ZOOKEEPER. Impossible, I'm afraid. Otherwise I wouldn't be here.

GALLERY DIRECTOR. But why?

ZOOKEEPER. As you'll be aware, certain colours make bulls—

GALLERY DIRECTOR. Surely there's little red at the zoo.

ZOOKEEPER. These are Egyptian bulls, with red eyes!

GALLERY DIRECTOR. What difference does that make?

ZOOKEEPER. It's the opposite colour which enrages them.

GALLERY DIRECTOR. The opposite colour?

ZOOKEEPER. They are sensitive to green. And as the green hedges will soon be eaten away, the green grass trampled—

GALLERY DIRECTOR. And the green roofs?

ZOOKEEPER. Can easily be painted another colour. In the zoo it's impossible to do entirely without green because of the other animals.

GALLERY DIRECTOR. And how do you envisage the roofs here being painted?

ZOOKEEPER. I'll leave that in your capable hands. You have years of experience with art, you have a feeling for colour.

GALLERY DIRECTOR. Yes, I know.

ZOOKEEPER (*standing up*). It's just struck midday.

GALLERY DIRECTOR. And the green of the bell-towers, the adjacent gardens, the rooftops?

ZOOKEEPER. I'll leave that all up to you. The public gardens on the west side will soon be adopted as the bulls' feeding area. And the monastery gardens to the east—

GALLERY DIRECTOR. I have no say over them.

ZOOKEEPER. That will change. And by the way it would be good to silence the monastery bells. Not just those bells in fact, all the bells, every bell-like sound in the wider area.

GALLERY DIRECTOR. That includes a lot of things.

ZOOKEEPER. The herd have their own bells. Any others could confuse them.

GALLERY DIRECTOR. These gardens were set out here because you could hear bells from towers miles away, from the churches on the far side of the river, beyond the city limits even—

ZOOKEEPER. The herd's bells will replace all that. Amply. And, finally, people will know where the sounds are coming from. As you will be explaining to the priests and sextons in the far-flung villages.

GALLERY DIRECTOR. You're not saying that I—

ZOOKEEPER. There's no one better equipped than yourself to make the request. Please silence the bells for the sake of the bulls. It confuses them.

GALLERY DIRECTOR. I think it's much more likely that the sloping aspect of these gardens is what might confuse them, if they are brought in from the top, and the topiary which resembles human figures!

ZOOKEEPER. There are much steeper pastures, and shrubs more closely resembling humans.

GALLERY DIRECTOR. And back to the issue of the colour green. What colour should it be replaced with?

ZOOKEEPER. Red, black, blue or yellow, as I said—

GALLERY DIRECTOR. My feeling for colour!

ZOOKEEPER. And for the herd's movements, which you will have to follow.

GALLERY DIRECTOR. How should I—

ZOOKEEPER. When you see the cattle crowding past the sphinxes and along the broad paths, your delight will overcome everything.

GALLERY DIRECTOR. I'm wondering how I'll explain that to the children who have played in the gardens till now—

ZOOKEEPER. They'll be thrilled to be bits by the bulls.

GALLERY DIRECTOR. And their grandmothers?

ZOOKEEPER. They will be as thrilled as their grandchildren. It will feel like a memory of something long lost, and their grand-children will sense a vision of the future. Anyone so much as casting a glance at their white backs will realize this is what they had always sought, no more gravel paths, topiary, sculptures, paintings, sublime yet poorly lit, no . . . just broad white backs in the sunlight, heads and horns, the whole herd—bulls!

GALLERY DIRECTOR. When all is this supposed to begin?

ZOOKEEPER. Very soon.

GALLERY DIRECTOR. You will inform me when the time comes?

ZOOKEEPER. Even if I don't come—

GALLERY DIRECTOR. I will have to start making space soon.

ZOOKEEPER. You will be remunerated.

GALLERY DIRECTOR. My position as director of these galleries—

ZOOKEEPER. Will be expanded to cover the surrounding streets, the roofs and towers, the adjoining gardens.

GALLERY DIRECTOR. Additional responsibilities.

ZOOKEEPER. Which in your shoes I would jump at.

GALLERY DIRECTOR. And later? When all the bells have been stilled, all the gardens grazed bare, when the green of the surrounding towers and cupulas has been obscured, when everyone unwill-ing to herd and feed cattle has been evicted from their homes, and when the bulls are crowding down the stone steps into the empty ponds, lit by the sun? When the shifting boundaries between their bodies are the only boundaries seen from here?

ZOOKEEPER. You will still have the windows half open as you have now.

GALLERY DIRECTOR. And me? What about me? When the galleries in the Upper and Lower Palaces have been stripped of paintings and sculptures, when I can no longer pick up my hat and step out to contemplate the treasures alone for a moment?

ZOOKEEPER. You will only be interested in the whiteness of the bulls, as I am now.

GALLERY DIRECTOR. Even in the evenings?

ZOOKEEPER. Even then. By then you may well be slightly blinded. Anyone who gazes for years at the vivid white herd eventually goes blind.

GALLERY DIRECTOR. I'm going to go blind?

ZOOKEEPER (*at the door*). Yes.

GALLERY DIRECTOR. Just to go back to the colour green, there are moments, such as before a storm, when the sky takes on a greenish tint. Occasionally in the evenings, too, as I said.

ZOOKEEPER. It can be a huge shock to the herd. It may trigger them to charge round in a circle.

GALLERY DIRECTOR. But how—

ZOOKEEPER. You will know how to prevent it.

GALLERY DIRECTOR. I do not think that in such a situation my feeling for colour would—

The Zookeeper has left.

GALLERY DIRECTOR. Years of experience with paintings . . . (*Walks to the window and looks up at the sky.*) Go green!

A child calls out to another. Birds sing. The sky is blue, with white clouds.

7

A Losing Battle

A TOY DRAGOON IN THE TOY MEADOW. Where am I going to be put?

TOY MAKER. In the foyer of a restaurant named after you.

DRAGOON. Along with the meadow?

TOY MAKER. Along with the meadow.

DRAGOON. What about the lighting?

TOY MAKER. Very natural. From eleven in the morning till eleven in the evening.

DRAGOON. And at night?

TOY MAKER. It's dark.

DRAGOON. What about my horse?

TOY MAKER. He's there too.

DRAGOON. What about the dampness from the river?

TOY MAKER. You can sense it.

DRAGOON. What about the mosquitos?

TOY MAKER. Likewise. There's a pond sketched out in the background. It looks like you've just been ferried across it. Now you're on watch.

DRAGOON. Yes, I know. Just now it was as if I heard footsteps from the thicket. But now—

TOY MAKER. Now you can't hear anything. OK?

DRAGOON. Yes.

TOY MAKER. Anything else?

DRAGOON. The air.

TOY MAKER. Barely noticeable. If at all, then only mixed with the strawberry scent of the frozen ground, the whiff of snow from the coats in the cloakroom, with—

DRAGOON. Who will see me?

TOY MAKER. Strangers mainly— (*Notices the Dragoon's unease.*) But also the girls from the ticket agency opposite, from the shoe shop in the lane off the Cathedral Square, from the delicatessen on the corner.

DRAGOON. And—

TOY MAKER. Anything else?

DRAGOON. Will no one notice how small I am?

TOY MAKER. I'm not sure what you mean.

DRAGOON. I mean, won't it surprise anyone?

TOY MAKER. No, because no one will expect anything different. Your appeal rests largely on it.

DRAGOON. To be honest I'd rather be walking in the 1910 Corpus Christi procession.

TOY MAKER. You have a much bigger role here. You're alone.

DRAGOON. Alone—

TOY MAKER. With the cracking from the bushes, at dawn, the enemy behind you—

DRAGOON. And if anyone realizes that the sun will never rise, the mosquitos never fly up?

TOY MAKER. They won't realize it; they'll already have assumed it.

DRAGOON. And that I'm expecting the enemy?

TOY MAKER. Don't worry what you're expecting. The guests' expectations are rather finer, the girls' expectations—

DRAGOON. Is my uniform up to scratch?

TOY MAKER. You look as much like yourself as you possibly can.

DRAGOON. That doesn't tell me much.

TOY MAKER. I've put a slight smirk on your face, a grin; whatever your audience sees won't be a surprise. They'll know there's no sky above the branches, they'll know—

DRAGOON. Yes, thank you. And if I want to set off and escape the dawn, escape my pretty meadow?

TOY MAKER. You can't. You're behind glass.

DRAGOON. Behind glass? (*Falls from his horse unconscious.*)

TOY MAKER (*shrinking*). Oi! Man up. Get back up. Get back on your horse. Don't let the grass grow. Don't let the enemy break through. Don't let the mosquitos fly up from the marsh. Don't let the sun rise! (*Now shrunk to the size of the Dragoon.*) Are you hurt?

The Toy Maker is stock-still.

DRAGOON. Have you been hit?

The Toy Maker remains immobile.

The mosquitos rise from the pond. The bushes start to rustle in the morning wind.

TOY MAKER (*suddenly realizes he is in an unfamiliar uniform*). Oh God! (*Tries to mount the Dragoon's horse, which becomes nervous.*) Come on!

The Dragoon stirs. Sighs.

The Toy Maker leaps over him, tries to get down to the river, hits the glass and disappears into the bushes.

DRAGOON (*waking up, raises himself on his arms*). I just thought I heard footsteps from the bushes. But now I can't hear anything.

He washes his face in the pond, swings up onto his horse and listens.

From now on everyone remains immobile.

8
Algebra

FRIEND. What if there was a sandstorm today?

GIRL. A sandstorm?

FRIEND. Yes.

GIRL. Now, in November?

FRIEND. It felt like it when I came through your hallway. It was warm and it smelt of fish.

GIRL. That's from the Italian restaurant on the ground floor.

FRIEND. And all bright, and the walls were covered in bright-green tiles.

GIRL. So the steam from the kitchen doesn't soak into the walls. It's all because of the restaurant.

FRIEND. Suddenly it looked like a sandstorm, a sandstorm where crabs fly through the windows and Californian monkeys swing through the streets, a fierce storm coming up from the Danube, a very fierce—

GIRL. Shall we get started on our maths. Fanny will bring the tea in a moment.

FRIEND. The kind of sandstorm which might knock the sun out of the sky, get rid of the smell of smoke or spoil the fun of Christmas. Which could make it bright as day now, at six—

GIRL. Half-seven.

FRIEND. Which would blow out the stars, mistaking them for lanterns, and smash the thick pane in the window of the dairy shop—

GIRL. Let's start with algebra.

FRIEND. A sandstorm—

In the kitchen.

THE COOK. Here's your supper, Jakob.

THE CRETIN. Yes.

COOK. It's not too hot.

CRETIN. No.

COOK. I blew on it to cool it down, with my own breath.

CRETIN. Yes.

COOK. But you don't know what 'my own breath' means.

CRETIN. No.

COOK. Don't spill it, will you. Not a drop.

CRETIN. Not a drop.

COOK. And don't go in to the girls, understand! With your huge head.

CRETIN. I won't either.

COOK. I'm going shopping now, to the dairy shop. Do you want to come?

The Cretin shakes his head.

COOK. That's for the best.

The door closes.

In the living room.

FRIEND. One which makes the monastery bells ring like ships' bells.

GIRL. We really need to get started—

FRIEND. Which blows the stone greyhounds off the gateway opposite.

GIRL. That's enough! If we don't get started soon—

FRIEND. Which—

GIRL. Where is your exercise book?

FRIEND. I've forgotten it.

GIRL. You've forgotten it!

FRIEND. A sandstorm which—

GIRL. Be quiet!

FRIEND. Which— (*Cries out loud.*)

GIRL. What's up?

FRIEND. Nothing.

GIRL. It's not nothing!

FRIEND. The door opened.

GIRL. The door?

FRIEND. And I saw a head behind you, a very large head—

GIRL. And?

FRIEND. Someone grinning.

GIRL. That was my brother.

FRIEND. I didn't know you even had a brother!

GIRL. I do. Shall we do our maths now?

FRIEND. Yes.

GIRL. I'll lend you an old exercise book.

    The scratching of pens.

9

First Semester

STUDENT (*a girl, not especially young*). I wanted to ask if you have any rooms available.

CONCIERGE (*she is not young either*). Rooms?

STUDENT. I heard there was a women's halls of residence here.

CONCIERGE. Our halls are fully occupied, or rather—

STUDENT. I have a character reference from the rector.

CONCIERGE. Where have you come from?

STUDENT. Two hours north of here on the train. You won't have heard of it. But our rector—

CONCIERGE. How long would you like to stay?

STUDENT. As long as possible, really.

CONCIERGE. As long as possible?

STUDENT. I mean, two or three years. No longer.

CONCIERGE. The halls are closed.

STUDENT. Closed? Didn't you just say—

CONCIERGE. That they are occupied?

STUDENT. Yes.

CONCIERGE. Precisely. They are indeed occupied.

STUDENT. I don't understand. You still have the sign above the entrance.

CONCIERGE. We're obliged to keep that.

STUDENT. And you're in the phone book under 'Women's Halls of Residence'.

CONCIERGE (*abruptly standing up straight and tall*). Closed in the immediate sense. Occupied in the everlasting.

STUDENT (*brows furrowed*). Which means—

CONCIERGE. That's the only sense they can be occupied in.

STUDENT (*excitedly*). So I could stay?

CONCIERGE. Yes, as I just said—

STUDENT. Would my rector be aware of these conditions?

CONCIERGE. I fear that in rectories two hours north of here by train ...Wouldn't you like to step inside?

STUDENT. I'd like to know what 'everlasting' means.

CONCIERGE. That's hard to explain on the doorstep.

STUDENT. Presumably, I'd have to stay in the first semester for ever?

CONCIERGE. In the current one certainly.

STUDENT. That's the first in my case. And in the same faculty?

CONCIERGE. In the one you first chose, yes.

STUDENT. That's the same thing. (*Thoughtful.*) I'm not sure my rector ...I don't have any travel money to go back home and ask him!

CONCIERGE. I'm sure your rector—

STUDENT. Our rector wants me to complete my studies and open a practice in our town.

CONCIERGE. I don't wish to put pressure on you, but it's started to rain. If you could decide soon—

STUDENT. But wouldn't I have to attend the same lectures, too?

CONCIERGE. That follows.

STUDENT. I mean, the exact same ones?

CONCIERGE. As you know, to God a thousand years are like a day.

STUDENT (*putting on a headscarf, hesitant*). Yes.

CONCIERGE. Well, as many lectures as you'd usually have that day. Five or six. Some of our residents have seminars too.

STUDENT. I probably won't, in my first semester.

CONCIERGE. No. Particularly unlikely as today is only the second day. But that has its advantages. You will be outdoors a lot. First thing in the morning you will always go for a walk in the small park near here.

STUDENT (*looks up*). Always under the same milky sky, in the same gentle rain?

CONCIERGE. Some people really like the gentle rain.

STUDENT. I'm sure. Back home I always used to—

CONCIERGE. And towards evening, from your room you will always see the same children in the lit-up windows opposite as they come home from their afternoon lessons. The little boy will sit down at the piano. And the girl will always—

STUDENT (*dreamily*). Then it will start raining harder and get dark. And that slight smell of smoke—

CONCIERGE. Will be in the air the whole time.

STUDENT. It's definitely raining harder now.

CONCIERGE. If you'd like to come in? We've got the heating on, even in the hallway.

STUDENT (*without yet setting foot inside*). Everywhere tiled blue?

CONCIERGE. Yes.

STUDENT. It's really very pretty. I'm wondering whether my rector—

CONCIERGE. White curtains in every room!

STUDENT. Whether my rector, if he could see what it was like here—

CONCIERGE. And central heating of course, flowers, fitted wardrobes!

STUDENT. He's always been at pains to ensure my welfare.

CONCIERGE. Well, he need have no further concerns.

STUDENT (*thoughtful*). No.

CONCIERGE. So, you see!

STUDENT. I'm just thinking—what about Christmas?

CONCIERGE. Oh, it's always equally soon without every actually coming. But anyway over the last few years— (*Smiles.*) when we still counted in years—it had started to get more and more commercial.

STUDENT (*to herself*). It's soon.

CONCIERGE. Yes, always this milky sky which leads to snow clouds. But it never snows. The shop windows haven't been decorated yet, but they soon will be.

STUDENT. I wanted to go home for Christmas.

CONCIERGE. You'll have no desire to.

STUDENT. No desire?

CONCIERGE. Because you'll just have come from home. This day has the advantage of not being too far from summer. It's actually the day the summer comes to fruition. You still have your home, fields, meadows, hay, in your thoughts—without them twisting your thoughts entirely.

STUDENT. There aren't many fields back home, but it's true. I was just thinking about it.

CONCIERGE. Everything is close.

STUDENT. Yes.

CONCIERGE. What are you still wondering?

STUDENT. Our rector—

CONCIERGE. You'll never be in danger of disappointing him. Your rector—

STUDENT. Will I always be wearing this blue hat? (*Reaches for her head.*)

CONCIERGE. Obviously. And you'll always meet children with similar hats on your walks!

STUDENT. Children, that's good!

CONCIERGE. Nice children, happy children! They'll walk past you laughing, their bags brushing against yours, whooping in the dusk.

STUDENT. Oh yes!

CONCIERGE. Step inside!

STUDENT (*hesitant, one foot on the doorstep*). But if I wanted to go and live somewhere else?

CONCIERGE. Somewhere else? I assume you don't have any relatives in the city.

STUDENT. If I still can't make up my mind, despite everything?

CONCIERGE. Then the rain falling on your coat now, will soon turn to snow. From this day on everything will unfold swiftly. Christmas will come and just as soon be over. Summer will come and hardly stay a moment!

STUDENT. But I will finish my degree?

CONCIERGE. The ten semesters will be over faster than a morning here with us, faster than the few lively, undemanding inaugural lectures you'd have to listen to.

STUDENT. And I will take over the practice in my hometown?

CONCIERGE. More likely you'd sink your arms for ever, weak and tired, as you return from your little walk in the gentle rain to drink a cup of tea and dry your clothes.

STUDENT. But our rector?

CONCIERGE. Your rector, who will always remain only two hours away by train—

STUDENT. Always.

CONCIERGE. Your rector would be long dead by then. What are you waiting for?

STUDENT. Oh, everything.

She withdraws her foot, the door to the women's halls of residence slams shut and it starts to snow in large, watery flakes.

10

Heavy Water

ELDERLY WOMAN. I'm walking in the rain here.

SECOND ELDERLY WOMAN. I saw it from my window— (*Looks up.*)

ELDERLY WOMAN. The rain brushes straight off this coat.

SECOND ELDERLY WOMAN (*touches the coat*). It really does.

ELDERLY WOMAN. And it looks even sleeker.

> *The Second Elderly Woman nods.*

ELDERLY WOMAN. That doesn't always look like the same word. (*Points to a red building in the distance.*)

SECOND ELDERLY WOMAN (*timidly*). No, it doesn't.

ELDERLY WOMAN. When it rains, it's 'chool', later—

SECOND ELDERLY WOMAN. From my window it reads as 'school'.

ELDERLY WOMAN. 'School'?

SECOND ELDERLY WOMAN. Yes, 'Girls' School'.

ELDERLY WOMAN (*testily*). And then it's just a question of whether the pigeons refrain from sullying my hat as soon as the rain eases off.

SECOND ELDERLY WOMAN (*touches the hat*). Felt?

ELDERLY WOMAN. Coarse felt, black marbled. The traditional technique.

SECOND ELDERLY WOMAN. Not so water-resistant?

ELDERLY WOMAN. Not at all.

SECOND ELDERLY WOMAN. Are the pigeons all right here?

ELDERLY WOMAN. Yes, everyone. (*Whispers.*) It's because of my hat.

SECOND ELDERLY WOMAN. To think it hadn't occurred to me yet.

ELDERLY WOMAN. Occurred to you?

Second Elderly Woman gestures to the school building with her head.

ELDERLY WOMAN. These things take time.

SECOND ELDERLY WOMAN. That really does help.

ELDERLY WOMAN. There are places to stand which help.

SECOND ELDERLY WOMAN. I'm totally soaked.

ELDERLY WOMAN. Your coat?

SECOND ELDERLY WOMAN. Yes.

ELDERLY WOMAN. It looked bright but heavy to me.

SECOND ELDERLY WOMAN. It lets water through.

ELDERLY WOMAN (*nods*). The heavy pieces, you know—

SECOND ELDERLY WOMAN. But my hat is light.

ELDERLY WOMAN. Makes you think. And then there's the pigeons, just waiting till it's over so they can land one on your head and shoulders. (*Points to the sky.*)

SECOND ELDERLY WOMAN. I almost feel I'm expecting them.

ELDERLY WOMAN. I'm not. When the sun's out I read it as 'ool'. That provides some cover. (*Pause.*) After a while it all calms down again.

SECOND ELDERLY WOMAN. The pigeons, too?

ELDERLY WOMAN. Fly right off.

SECOND ELDERLY WOMAN. And me? I can't exchange flats, not now. (*Frowning.*) 'Girls' School'—'Girls' School'?

ELDERLY WOMAN. Up in the sky.

SECOND ELDERLY WOMAN (*worried*). Quite soon?

ELDERLY WOMAN. The sun.

ELDERLY WOMAN. Soon?

ELDERLY WOMAN. Even sooner, it'll all calm down again.

11

The Auction

AUCTIONEER. Next up is a piece of blue sky and a chest of drawers.

HECKLER. From today?

WOMAN. The chest of drawers is from today. The blue sky is from the day before yesterday around eleven when two trams collided near the old hospital.

Silence.

AUCTIONEER. I also have plot of woodland from the year 1604 on the site where today part of the new prison—

WOMAN (*wearing a ragged fur*). I bid a rabbit.

AUCTIONEER. Dead or alive?

WOMAN. Alive.

AUCTIONEER. What for?

WOMAN. For the blue sky the day before yesterday around eleven when two trams collided near the hospital—

AUCTIONEER. The old hospital.

WOMAN. The old hospital—

AUCTIONEER (*interrupting her*). One rabbit for the blue sky. Going— (*Interrupts himself.*) I should remind you that all the blue in the sky from the day before yesterday around eleven will become this woman's property if no one—

HECKLER. Heckling is forbidden!

AUCTIONEER. Going!

MAN (*in a sleek, black coat*). I bid the old theatre.

The Woman starts crying.

AUCTIONEER. Open or closed?

MAN. Closed.

AUCTIONEER. What for?

The Woman cries louder.

MAN (*giving her a sympathetic look*). For the woodland plot from 1604.

AUCTIONEER (*sternly*). The lot in question is the blue sky.

MAN. My apologies.

AUCTIONEER (*softening*). So you'd like it then?

MAN. No. For the old theatre I exchanged a hereditary lease on the playground at the girls' grammar school from the year 2000 onwards. Now I'd like the woodland from 1604 for the old theatre. I can reasonably expect rabbits.

HECKLER. If I were you—

AUCTIONEER. I must ask for quiet. I am still auctioning the blue sky.

WOMAN (*whispering to the woman sitting next to her*). My son was injured in the crash you see. He was on the platform waiting for the tram behind!

AUCTIONEER (*monotonously*). May I remind you that all blue in the sky from the day before yesterday around eleven, the blue over the pawnbrokers and the blue over the ocean, will become this woman's property if no one—

HECKLER (*speaking quietly to the Man*). If I were you I would let her have the blue and then auction the rabbit!

MAN. That's just what I was thinking.

AUCTIONEER. Going. For the last time!

WOMAN (*to her neighbour*). The doctors have given me cause for hope. But I thought, just in case!

AUCTIONEER. Going. Think carefully!

NEIGHBOURING WOMAN. Will you have it framed?

The Woman nods energetically.

AUCTIONEER. Gone. (*To the Woman, sullenly*) You may collect it.

The Woman disappears into a dark side-room, first handing the rabbit to the Auctioneer.

AUCTIONEER (*despondent, holding the rabbit by its scruff*). The sky has ended up in the wrong hands now.

HECKLER (*enthusiastically*). All the woods!

NEIGHBOURING WOMAN (*offended*). Your son works for the Taxman.

AUCTIONEER. The remaining lots are—a chest of drawers and a plot of woodland from the year 1604—

HECKLER. What about the rabbit?

AUCTIONEER. It hasn't been valued yet.

MAN (*in a sleek, black coat*). I bid the performance at the old theatre from the eleventh of November 1897!

AUCTIONEER. Which kind?

MAN. Operetta.

AUCTIONEER. Which operetta?

MAN. I no longer recall.

AUCTIONEER. What for?

MAN. For the rabbit.

AUCTIONEER. I'm currently auctioning the plot of woodland.

MAN. Ah I see.

AUCTIONEER. You knew perfectly well!

MAN. I'm a painter and I live in a quiet spot. I'm interested in the rabbit.

The Auctioneer shakes his head.

MAN. I could also offer a complementary ticket to a school play in September 2003. One of the many perks of my job.

AUCTIONEER. Which— (*Interrupts himself.*) For the rabbit?

The Man nods.

AUCTIONEER (*absent-minded*). The remaining lots are—one chest of drawers, one plot of woodland from 1604—

HECKLER (*with a cry of scorn*). And?

AUCTIONEER (*takes a deep breath*). The rails from three children's beds from the infectious diseases ward.

HECKLER. I knew he was holding something back.

AUCTIONEER (*without letting himself be put off*). Previously used in a private household, later passed on to the children's hospital.

MAN (*in a sleek coat*). I'll take it.

AUCTIONEER. And you're bidding?

MAN. A banister, highly polished.

HECKLER. A crate of oranges. Freshly picked!

The Auctioneer shakes his head.

MAN (*unimpressed*). Whatever you want.

AUCTIONEER. That is not sufficient.

MAN (*takes a deep breath*). An invitation to a children's tea party— girls. Early autumn, 1911. Near here, but it never took place because one of the girls died of scarlet fever two days earlier.

AUCTIONEER (*sternly*). The girl—did she go to school?

MAN. She did.

AUCTIONEER. The autumn leaves?

MAN. Were swirling.

AUCTIONEER. The hatbands?

MAN. Flew off.

AUCTIONEER. And were they bright?

MAN. Enough!

AUCTIONEER. I'd still like to know the location.

MAN. Close to the old theatre, perhaps northwest of it. The storey number was on a sign over the door, to the right. It was shiny.

AUCTIONEER (*thoughtful, holding his notebook*). Northwest— Above the door—

MAN. It was approaching three.

AUCTIONEER. I should like to point out that the rails I am auctioning were leant up outside for four years, facing west–northwest and simultaneously east—

WOMAN. That fits.

AUCTIONEER. On top of a plane-tree crown.

Silence.

AUCTIONEER. Is no one bidding any more? (*Animated, insecure.*) I know my strengths. I once made a great effort to save an umbrella shop from— I saved it—

HECKLER. Why?

AUCTIONEER. A shop with musical instruments!

MAN (*to himself*). The play of sunlight.

AUCTIONEER. A very special, highly rated one. You know it?

The Man nods.

AUCTIONEER (*sternly*). The smell of Lysol?

MAN. Wore off as the coats swished.

AUCTIONEER. Where did the coats swish?

MAN. On the road south, passing three gardens.

AUCTIONEER. Didn't the bells ring the hour then? (*Insistent.*) Did the bells ring?

MAN (*shakes his head, hesitant*). Her heart missed a beat at three.

AUCTIONEER. You can collect it. (*Drops his arms and releases the rabbit, which leaps onto the window sill.*) Would you like it instead of the white rails?

The rabbit jumps three storeys down into the courtyard.

MAN (*leans out of the window and looks down*). For God's sake!

AUCTIONEER. I hereby end the auction.

The Heckler sobs.

The bells ring three o'clock.

12

Good Sea

CASHIER AT THE CINEMA. Nets blocking the entrance. Yet again.

A PASSING POLICEMAN. So what will you do with them?

The Cashier shrugs.

POLICEMAN. If they were fishing nets—

CASHIER. Yes.

POLICEMAN. That would mean good luck in the morning.

CASHIER *(sarcastically)*. Shark nets, tuna nets, dried-cod nets—

POLICEMAN. And always graded?

CASHIER *(nods)*. I'm going to open up.

POLICEMAN *(approaching, curious)*. Which is it today?

CASHIER. Shark.

POLICEMAN. Shark!

CASHIER *(while carefully removing the net from the doorway, to herself)*.
Good sea—good sail—good soul—

POLICEMAN. I can hear perfectly well.

CASHIER. Five little ducks at seven in the morning, and the filthy
linen rags—

POLICEMAN. I can hear you.

CASHIER. Got to take care it doesn't catch on the corner.

POLICEMAN. Of course!

CASHIER. Otherwise there's no point.

POLICEMAN (*eagerly*). You can tell, by the way, the sky whips the leaves off the trees on the avenue.

CASHIER (*as if holding needles between her lips*). Mhm.

POLICEMAN. So effortless and so fast!

CASHIER. Practice!

> *She takes the net down and places it carefully over her arm. The Policeman watches as she unlocks the outer metal gate.*

POLICEMAN. And now?

CASHIER. I'll put it with the others.

> *She unlocks her kiosk and places it inside.*

POLICEMAN. Good stuff.

CASHIER. I'm supposed to be at the hairdresser's by two.

POLICEMAN. The hairdresser's?

CASHIER. Maybe I'll hand them all over to him . . . (*Pointing to the pile of nets.*)

POLICEMAN. What for?

CASHIER. A dark place—artificial light all year round. A lot of uses for nets!

POLICEMAN. Easy to find.

CASHIER. As easy as not.

POLICEMAN (*bites his lip*). Not frayed at all!

CASHIER (*sarcastically*). Perhaps, I should go to the lost-property office. So the sea becomes easier to catch.

POLICEMAN. I think not.

CASHIER. They have greener pastures there!

POLICEMAN. I know.

CASHIER. Tailors' pastures, for instance.

POLICEMAN. I know.

The Cashier strokes the nets gently.

POLICEMAN. How it rustles.

CASHIER. With no guarantee.

POLICEMAN. Without anything at all.

CASHIER. It's worth something.

POLICEMAN. I pictured shark nets coarser than this.

CASHIER. Me too. But there are lampshade-makers' pastures, opera pastures, confectioners' pastures—there you soon learn they have to be fine.

POLICEMAN. Shark-ha!

The Cashier looks at him, amazed.

POLICEMAN (*seeing the nets, shudders*). It's growing!

CASHIER. What else would it do?

POLICEMAN (*insistent*). And you?

CASHIER. I just said. (*Squeezes in by the nets.*)

POLICEMAN. Just one, if I could have one!

CASHIER (*coolly*). That would be very straightforward.

POLICEMAN. Shark or squid—I could go either way!

CASHIER. I don't doubt it, then go and catch the kids messing around before three.

The Policeman remains silent.

CASHIER. Right?

POLICEMAN. I don't want to catch anything. I'll let the ducks swim and the children ride home from school on the buses.

CASHIER. And?

POLICEMAN. I'll let the white beneath leaves be called silver—as it were—

CASHIER (*assuaged*). That would be a good start.

POLICEMAN. 'The dusk gold.'

CASHIER. As it were.

POLICEMAN. I won't interrupt any maths lessons or exercises or any lessons in any languages. I'll leave the cars parked off to the left of all the schools, freshly washed.

The Cashier nods.

POLICEMAN. Then I'll turn back—

CASHIER. And, and?

POLICEMAN. And lie down at seven in the morning in the filthy linen shrouds the dead have just risen from.

CASHIER. And?

POLICEMAN. Turn around and hold the net in both hands.

CASHIER. And?

POLICEMAN. Catch myself.

13

Return

The doorbell rings at an out-of-the-way ship chandler's and fishing shop.

FIRST SAILOR. Hands up!

SECOND SAILOR. Although we come unarmed.

THIRD SAILOR. I'll watch the door.

AN OLD MAN (*proprietor of the shop*). What—

FIRST SAILOR. You know full well.

OLD MAN. Can I help?

SECOND SAILOR. Do you not remember?

THIRD SAILOR. Three years ago you sold us some lifebuoys.

OLD MAN. I sell a lot of lifebuoys.

FIRST SAILOR. They were no good.

OLD MAN. I don't recall a thing.

FIRST SAILOR. It was a hot day.

SECOND SAILOR. Midday, like today.

THIRD SAILOR. You had nothing left in the storeroom so you fetched
the buoys from the window.

OLD MAN. I don't remember.

THIRD SAILOR. There were exactly three there.

SECOND SAILOR. They were no good.

OLD MAN. I don't know what you're talking about.

THIRD SAILOR. We're talking about that day.

SECOND SAILOR. A Sunday.

FIRST SAILOR. You were open.

SECOND SAILOR. We were pleased you were open.

FIRST SAILOR. When we came in we were still dazzled from the sunlight.

OLD MAN. And?

SECOND SAILOR. The doorbell tinkled like today.

THIRD SAILOR. We asked for the lifebuoys and you gave them to us.

FIRST SAILOR. The three lifebuoys in the window.

SECOND SAILOR. Dusty lifebuoys. But you said, 'When push comes to shove, the deluge will rinse them clean.'

OLD MAN. Did I?

SECOND SAILOR. Yes. We were content with that.

OLD MAN. I say that quite often when I sell lifebuoys. It's meant to bring good luck.

FIRST SAILOR. We thought so too.

SECOND SAILOR. The night still rang in our ears like music.

THIRD SAILOR. We went cheerfully off.

OLD MAN. All my lifebuoys are dusty.

SECOND SAILOR. The deluge washed them clean.

FIRST SAILOR. But otherwise—

THIRD SAILOR. They were no good.

OLD MAN. It is possible the lifebuoys in the window were slightly bleached from the sun.

SECOND SAILOR. That too—

THIRD SAILOR. But that wasn't all.

FIRST SAILOR. They were too heavy.

OLD MAN. I'll take it up with my supplier!

FIRST SAILOR. Perhaps they were only intended for a shop window—

SECOND SAILOR. Yes, perhaps—

THIRD SAILOR. We didn't notice straight away.

SECOND SAILOR. Perhaps they were only a little heavier.

THIRD SAILOR. When the ship sank, they didn't float.

FIRST SAILOR. That was a sunny day, too.

SECOND SAILOR. The Caribbean Sea!

THIRD SAILOR. We were crossing it for the first time.

SECOND SAILOR. The sharks!

OLD MAN. Perhaps you didn't have the lifebuoys round your bodies properly.

SECOND SAILOR. We had them on right.

OLD MAN. Perhaps you didn't hold on to them hard enough!

SECOND SAILOR. Hard enough!

OLD MAN. Perhaps the sharks tore them off!

THIRD SAILOR. They only came later.

OLD MAN. Who can say?

FIRST SAILOR. We can.

SECOND SAILOR. Today, the day of our resurrection—

OLD MAN. Have mercy on me!

FIRST SAILOR. Too sunny to ascend into heaven.

THIRD SAILOR. But calm enough.

SECOND SAILOR. We wanted to—

OLD MAN. By the mercy of God—who will soon receive you—leave me in peace!

SECOND SAILOR. We want to return the lifebuoys to you.

THIRD SAILOR. They are too heavy to take up with us.

OLD MAN. Where are they?

FIRST SAILOR. Lying on the jetty.

SECOND SAILOR. Where we emerged.

THIRD SAILOR. Come on!

On the jetty. At a distance, smoke rises from ships setting out to sea.

FIRST SAILOR. Here!

OLD MAN (*almost pleased*). There they are! I never thought I'd see them again.

THIRD SAILOR. Nor did we.

OLD MAN. So fresh and shiny.

SECOND SAILOR. As we emerged the seaweed slid off them!

THIRD SAILOR. The mud stayed below.

OLD MAN. Bright white, not a grain of dust.

FIRST SAILOR. No.

OLD MAN. What a glowing red the red stripes are. Even I never knew that.

Silence. The sun disappears.

OLD MAN (*strokes the lifebuoys fondly*). And the blue inscription—ES.

SECOND SAILOR. What does it stand for?

OLD MAN. Emergency Service—it's the brand.

THIRD SAILOR. I see.

OLD MAN. Not a fracture point.

The gloom intensifies. Wind builds up.

FIRST SAILOR. I'm getting chilly.

SECOND SAILOR. We can ascend soon.

OLD MAN. And you want to—you really want to return these?

THIRD SAILOR. Yes.

OLD MAN. And I don't have to pay anything for them?

SECOND SAILOR. No.

OLD MAN. I can take them back as if I'd never sold them?

The Sailors nod.

OLD MAN. And do what I want with them?

The First Sailor shoves his lifebuoy half off the edge of the jetty with his foot.

OLD MAN. What are you doing?

FIRST SAILOR. It nearly fell back in . . .

OLD MAN. God forbid!

SECOND SAILOR (*looks up at the sky*). It's going to be a cloudy Sunday.

THIRD SAILOR. I pictured the day of my resurrection rather differently.

SECOND SAILOR. The sun's not going to come out again, but it's calm still.

FIRST SAILOR. Time to ascend!

They rise to heaven.

OLD MAN (*puts his hands over his eyes, calls after them*). I remain indebted to you!

Shoves the lifebuoys under his arm, hobbles down the jetty towards the city and back to his shop.

Doorbell rings.

OLD MAN (*calling into the empty room*). It's only me.

He places the lifebuoys back in the shop window.

14

Through the Fresh Greenery

SEVERIN. A short street in my honour!

HIS COMPANION (*nods*). You were well aware.

SEVERIN. And who is it here we're—

COMPANION. An old woman.

SEVERIN. Alone? Suitable for questioning?

COMPANION. Alone. With a view of the treetops. The ice-cream par-
lours all around here are closing. (*Pushes open a door, entering a
block of flats.*) Anything else?

SEVERIN (*climbing the stairs*). I wanted— (*Thoughtful.*) Nothing. I
wanted it to be later that we—

The Companion rings the doorbell. Sound of footsteps inside.

COMPANION. Let me do the talking!

OLD WOMAN (*searching for her key*). Who's out there?

SEVERIN. We're from—

COMPANION. From the Association for Independent Opinion
Polling.

OLD WOMAN. I'm not a member.

COMPANION. Precisely! Those are the only people we canvas.

SEVERIN. You've been chosen—

COMPANION (*gives him an angry look*). Your parish priest recommended you to us.

OLD WOMAN (*holding the door ajar*). He didn't tell me you were coming. And he knows today's not a good day.

COMPANION. He didn't know it would be today. He just knew that around this time—

OLD WOMAN. I've never heard of your association.

COMPANION. We wanted to introduce ourselves. We are publicly funded. (*Pulls a piece of paper from his coat pocket.*)

OLD WOMAN (*hesitant, without looking at it*). Come in, if you like. But I'm in a hurry!

SEVERIN (*enters timidly, murmuring his name*). Good evening!

OLD WOMAN. Is it that late already? Just now I could still hear the kids from the street below.

SEVERIN (*staying still, awkward*). There's no sound from the kids any more.

OLD WOMAN. This way. I've just made tea. (*Places chairs in the oriel window.*) Tell me about your independent opinion polling? What's it all about?

SEVERIN. About everything.

COMPANION (*hastily*). Not just about opinions. Habits and activities, too—

OLD WOMAN. Habits? Activities?

COMPANION. Insofar as the opinions derive from them.

OLD WOMAN (*perturbed*). But I mustn't make myself late. (*Pours the tea.*) I'm going to a talk tonight.

COMPANION. A talk?

OLD WOMAN. 'Saint Severin and His Companion'.

SEVERIN (*agitated*). His companion—

OLD WOMAN. You're clearly not familiar with the subject.

COMPANION. I wouldn't say that. But it sounds as if it's part of a series.

OLD WOMAN (*nods*). A series, yes. I attend them along with my niece.

COMPANION. Your niece—

OLD WOMAN. It's a great excuse for us to see each other. We arrange to meet a few minutes before. (*Looks at the clock.*) After the talk she walks some of the way home with me.

COMPANION. And you discuss what you've just heard.

OLD WOMAN. Yes . . . (*Looks at him keenly.*) We discuss what we've heard. (*Shifts her glance.*) Sometimes we go another stop on foot. On warm evenings, sometimes, I find myself right on the corner here, red-cheeked, immersed in words—totally immersed—as if I were young again! Do you know what I'm saying?

COMPANION. The talks are weekly, aren't they?

OLD WOMAN (*nods*). Weekly.

COMPANION (*holding a notebook*). Seven left before summer.

OLD WOMAN. Seven left.

SEVERIN. No.

OLD WOMAN. Yes, seven.

SEVERIN. There aren't seven left.

OLD WOMAN. How many then?

COMPANION. Seven, rest assured.

OLD WOMAN (*smiling*). My niece and I must have got it wrong. The whole time we've been assuming the series runs till the end of June, till the start of summer!

COMPANION. That's exactly how long it runs.

OLD WOMAN. After that we wanted to go on holiday, not too far, not too long—

COMPANION. And in the autumn you'll sign up for another series?

OLD WOMAN. Yes. I've been going to talks for years. They stimulate your mind, and keep you informed.

COMPANION. And do you let the speakers know they have this effect?

OLD WOMAN. I do. I often write letters to them. It helps while away the evenings when my niece isn't here.

COMPANION. Even in the brighter months?

OLD WOMAN. The last few weeks have encouraged me no end. After walking through the fresh greenery, the words come to me in an instant!

SEVERIN. There aren't seven talks left.

OLD WOMAN. But you can read it. It's been advertised.

COMPANION. You'll never convince him.

OLD WOMAN. Bright-green posters!

Severin shakes his head.

COMPANION. See what I mean— And next summer?

OLD WOMAN. A trip. A tour organized by some of the speakers.

COMPANION. And next autumn?

OLD WOMAN. Then we wanted to— (*Hesitates, then smiles.*) —Well, go to the talks again.

COMPANION. And the summer after?

OLD WOMAN. Holidays! And, perhaps, I'll eventually move in with my niece—

COMPANION. And the autumn after next?

OLD WOMAN. Talks. (*Still smiling.*) Really, when I consider the future, I just see us walking beneath the trees discussing the talks we've just heard!

SEVERIN. There aren't seven trees left.

COMPANION. And the summer after that?

OLD WOMAN (*thoughtful, furrowing her brows*). The summer?

SEVERIN. No summers left!

COMPANION. But the autumn after?

OLD WOMAN (*leaning back*). All I can see is—black–green, black–green, black–green. I feel dizzy! If I miss the talk today, it'll be the fault of your questions!

SEVERIN (*leaning towards her, emphatically*). There is no talk!

OLD WOMAN (*frightened, to the Companion*). You know, don't you! You can see me walking down a grey street which ends with trees, perhaps stooping more, less animated, but it's me! You know what will happen that autumn, in two autumns' time!

SEVERIN. There are no autumns left! (*He stands up.*)

COMPANION. Lots of autumns.

OLD WOMAN. One of you—

COMPANION. What will you do in the third autumn from now?

OLD WOMAN (*arduously*). What will I do in the third autumn from— in the third autumn from now—what will I do in the third autumn— (*Numb, losing her grip.*) In the third autumn from today—

COMPANION. What will you do then?

SEVERIN (*stands behind the Old Woman*). There aren't seven words left.

OLD WOMAN. I will— (*Thinks with difficulty.*)

COMPANION (*facing the Old Woman*). You know!

SEVERIN. You don't know!

COMPANION (*leans down close to the Old Woman, speaking into her ear*). Walk through the fresh greenery—you will walk through the

fresh greenery with your niece—through the fresh greenery—
the fresh greenery—repeat after me—walk through the fresh
greenery—

OLD WOMAN (*straightening up, calmly*). I don't know.

*Severin closes her eyes, takes her in his arms, walks past the Companion
and down the stairs.*

15

Sunday Shift

A Stewardess on the London–Johannesburg flight walks slowly down the dim corridor of the neurology clinic and knocks on a Junior Doctor's door.

STEWARDESS. Good evening.

DOCTOR. Is it that late already? I thought perhaps . . . The morning slipped into afternoon so quickly today. When you're not forced to stick to mealtimes you lose all sense of day and night!

STEWARDESS. It's nearly four.

DOCTOR. I just opened the window to feed the sparrows.

STEWARDESS. I saw. I was walking up the path from the park.

DOCTOR. But they weren't terribly hungry. It's mild enough today to let them forage for themselves. I'm glad you came. I don't like these days when I'm on duty but it feels like I'm off.

STEWARDESS. That's why I'm here.

DOCTOR. In a way you're relieving me from myself. Come in! Take a seat. And forgive me, I forgot to introduce myself—

STEWARDESS. I know you.

DOCTOR (*cheerfully*). My face probably. And I have the feeling I've seen you before in the corridor. You were waiting for someone.

STEWARDESS. I was waiting for you.

DOCTOR. For me?

STEWARDESS. It was a Sunday like today, and you were on duty. A bright day. Then you were called. (*Hesitates.*) A pity.

DOCTOR (*impatient*). Now you've found me.

STEWARDESS. It was better flying weather that day.

DOCTOR. You are the patient who was referred to me? My four o'clock appointment? (*Looks at the clock.*)

STEWARDESS. I work on the London–Johannesburg flight.

DOCTOR. This city is quite out of your way then.

STEWARDESS. It's on my flight path.

DOCTOR. And this clinic is a long way from the airport.

STEWARDESS. I can get here easily, at this time—

DOCTOR. It's not yet four.

STEWARDESS. And at this altitude.

DOCTOR. At which altitude?

STEWARDESS. Of the moment you flung the window open and felt off-duty although you weren't.

DOCTOR. And what latitude is this moment at?

STEWARDESS. At the latitude of the Atlantic, around four thousand metres above sea level.

DOCTOR. That's not very precise.

STEWARDESS (*eagerly*). I could be more precise if you wanted, the exact latitude—

DOCTOR. Thank you. The moment is too pointless, and the clouds above the infection pavilion are racing too fast. The sky here is high one minute, low the next. The sun, one minute as if it might shine, the next as if it won't.

STEWARDESS. The latitude to the exact thousandth.

DOCTOR. Too pointless for all that precision.

STEWARDESS (*more insistent*). We've passed Southampton, half an hour ago—

DOCTOR (*smiling for a moment*). So we won't be landing there any more?

The Stewardess shakes her head.

DOCTOR. Don't go to any more trouble. I'll be working here many more years. And not even the sparrows I feed will recognize me.

STEWARDESS. Everything can be identified.

DOCTOR. What good is that to me when I can't identify anything myself any more?

STEWARDESS. Precisely then.

DOCTOR. What do you want?

STEWARDESS (*nervous*). I haven't been on duty long.

DOCTOR. Are you experiencing anxiety?

STEWARDESS. I have been recently.

DOCTOR. When did it start?

STEWARDESS. On the twenty-third of August.

DOCTOR. The twenty-third of August?

STEWARDESS. A Sunday. I was on duty.

DOCTOR. I probably was, too.

STEWARDESS. Since then I've felt anxious every Sunday I have to work.

DOCTOR. But not otherwise?

STEWARDESS. No. And not all day either. Just from three till six.

DOCTOR. That's quite brief.

STEWARDESS (*hesitant again*). It happens every time.

DOCTOR (*affably*). And the morning, the afternoon? Weekdays?

The Stewardess shakes her head.

DOCTOR. That's excellent!

STEWARDESS (*imploring*). You know what Sundays from three to six mean, how long it is just till four.

DOCTOR. What seems to ease it?

STEWARDESS. We have the same shift plan—every third Sunday, sometimes just a fortnightly. It rotates according to a particular pattern.

DOCTOR. You soon got the hang of it.

STEWARDESS. If you're afraid—

DOCTOR. And before the twenty-third of August?

STEWARDESS. Then I had time. Every weekday, and Sunday morning too. We took off at three.

DOCTOR. Were you afraid?

STEWARDESS. Not immediately. But for the first time at four thousand metres I noticed it was Sunday. And that the direction we were flying in left little hope we would reach Monday.

DOCTOR. I know the feeling.

STEWARDESS. Just before four, I was instructed to initiate emergency procedures.

DOCTOR. And when—

STEWARDESS. It wasn't till after six that we went down. Into a riverbank, into the mud. The plane caught fire.

DOCTOR. On the twenty-third of August soon after six—

STEWARDESS. You picked up your hat and walked into town.

DOCTOR. That's possible. I can't remember any more.

STEWARDESS. I remember.

DOCTOR. Why did you come here?

STEWARDESS. Because I helped eleven people out of the fire, but not the twelfth. I pushed in front of him.

DOCTOR. Since then—

STEWARDESS. I've been looking for him ever since.

DOCTOR. The treatment here—

STEWARDESS (*quickly*). I wanted to ask you to cover my shift from three to six.

DOCTOR. When?

STEWARDESS. Just on the Sundays you're on duty and you feed the sparrows, when no one comes. (*As the Doctor is hesitant.*) That's unusual for you but this happens to me all the time.

DOCTOR. What does the job consist of?

STEWARDESS. Between three and four of unease. Later of fear. At six I can be relied on to take over.

DOCTOR (*thoughtful*). Haven't I covered your shifts several times before?

STEWARDESS. Sometimes. Now I'm asking you.

DOCTOR. And for how long?

STEWARDESS. Till I succeed in letting the twelfth go first. Till I have caught that moment and rid the world of those three hours. (*The Doctor remains hesitant.*) Till I have confronted the flames and the quagmire, fresh like a child waking from a deep sleep and still seeing angels! It's not chance that we have the same shift plan.

DOCTOR (*nodding*). We shouldn't leave it to chance.

She has left.

16
Doves and Wolves

GIRL. Good evening.

SECTARIAN (*sorting out food on an old, dark dining table*). Good evening.

GIRL. I was told to come here.

SECTARIAN. Do you have the card with you?

GIRL. Yes. That's where it said to come here. (*Starts looking for it, rummaging in her bag, finally finds it.*) Here!

SECTARIAN. Some people forget them, you see. It makes things complicated.

GIRL. Not me.

SECTARIAN. You've been chosen to receive a free food package.

GIRL. Yes?

SECTARIAN. And also some woollen clothes.

GIRL. That's wonderful. It's very cold.

SECTARIAN. You could have had it earlier, but I get the items from California. Sometimes there are delays.

SECTARIAN'S WIFE (*from the next room*). Are you nearly finished, Friedrich?

SECTARIAN. Almost done.

WIFE. Soon?

SECTARIAN. Very soon.

GIRL. I didn't think I'd get anything at all.

SECTARIAN. Our HQ is in California.

GIRL. I don't know anyone in California anyway.

SECTARIAN. The HQ doesn't make the selection.

GIRL. Oh I see.

SECTARIAN. I make the selection.

WIFE. You'll really be done soon, Friedrich?

GIRL. Really, very soon.

WIFE. Hurry up—but don't rush it!

GIRL (*fearful*). I don't know you either.

SECTARIAN. Are you in need?

GIRL. Oh yes.

SECTARIAN. That's what matters.

GIRL. But—

SECTARIAN (*tying up the cardboard box*). Each package contains two kilograms of rice, three bars of chocolate—they can also be used as drinking chocolate—four cans of condensed milk and a woollen waistcoat.

GIRL. Thank you very much!

SECTARIAN. Our HQ is in California.

WIFE. Finished, Friedrich?

SECTARIAN. In a minute. (*To the Girl.*) My wife runs a poultry farm.

WIFE. It's nearly three.

SECTARIAN. We always go there at three.

GIRL. Poultry?

SECTARIAN. Yes, rare birds—doves with white spurs, pheasants, all kinds of chicken. Once we had an ostrich, too.

GIRL. An ostrich?

SECTARIAN. If you want you can come with us!

The Girl hesitates.

SECTARIAN. I'm guessing you need to catch the tram.

GIRL. Yes.

SECTARIAN. It's on the way. (*Calls into the next room.*) Are you coming, Leonie?

WIFE. I'm coming.

Outside the house, continuing on the way to the poultry farm.

GIRL. I still don't know why—

SECTARIAN. Allow me to carry the box for you till we get there!

WIFE. Windy day today.

GIRL. I've been past here lots of times but—

SECTARIAN. On the train I'm guessing?

GIRL. Yes, on the train. And I've noticed your house, set back a little, next to the brickworks, with white curtains in the windows, with the fence—(*The other two are silent. The Girl appears somewhat dazed.*)—because it's so small—(*The others remain silent.*) When you pass by, it looks like a nice place to live but—

WIFE (*sharply*). But?

GIRL. From the train you can see the river and the house. So you assume that from the house you must be able to see the river and the train too.

WIFE. You only see the train.

GIRL. Yes. (*As if collecting herself.*) But I wanted to say something else.

SECTARIAN. We turn here.

GIRL. I wanted to ask—

WIFE. We've reached the coal yards now.

GIRL. I've seen your house from the train, travelling to work and back, and sometimes I think, this would be a nice place to live. But it's not possible that's the actual reason you— (*Stutters.*) That for that reason it was me you— (*Looks askance at the box.*)

SECTARIAN. You must have seen the coal yards, too.

GIRL (*dispirited*). Yes.

WIFE. Our poultry farm is in amongst them.

The Girl is silent.

WIFE. You'd never guess it.

GIRL (*dazed, like before, when she was talking about the river*). I once saw a white dove flying over the coal yards. It circled around in a wide arc then turned back. I was surprised. I wondered, why—

WIFE. It was bound to be one of ours.

GIRL. Yes, probably.

WIFE. They all do it at first.

GIRL. At first?

WIFE. No one can stop them flying over the coal yards and getting their wings all dirty.

SECTARIAN. Some of them even fly across the river to the squalid houses there.

WIFE. We can't hang a net under the sky.

SECTARIAN (*laughs*). It wouldn't be worth it anyway!

WIFE. After a while they stop of their own accord.

SECTARIAN. After a while.

WIFE. They realize our birdseed is nicer than that coal dust you crunch underfoot the whole time round here.

SECTARIAN. Or the sand lodged between the roof-tiles over there.

GIRL (*uneasy*). I can well imagine it's better.

WIFE. Yes, indeed. It's not hard to imagine.

Cries coming up from the river.

GIRL. What's that?

WIFE. Nothing.

SECTARIAN. Children playing on the barge down there.

WIFE. Scrapping.

FIRST CHILD (*far away, but clear*). Who's afraid of snow and ice?

OTHER CHILDREN. Not us!

FIRST CHILD. Who likes snow and ice?

CHILDREN. We do!

FIRST CHILD. Who's seen wolves?

CHILDREN. We have!

Pounding feet on wood as they run off. The voices recede.

GIRL. Wolves?

SECTARIAN. They always play that down there on the barge.

WIFE. They can't help it.

SECTARIAN. Ever since two wolves were once seen on the opposite bank of the river.

GIRL. Real wolves?

SECTARIAN. Probably a trick of the light.

WIFE. A rumour.

SECTARIAN. It's a long time ago.

GIRL. I've never heard about it. (*To the Sectarian.*) But you should really let me carry the box—really—

SECTARIAN. When the time comes.

GIRL. You've been carrying it so long! Not only did you give it to me in the first place, you're carrying it for me as well! And I still don't know why—

SECTARIAN. You are keeping us company in return.

GIRL. Why—

WIFE. We're nearly there.

GIRL. I mean, why do it at all, why choose me, why give it to me— Oh this wind! (*Brushes her hair out of her face.*)

WIFE. We're nearly there now!

GIRL. I didn't come this way. I came a different way.

WIFE. But it can't have been far from where you saw the dove, am I right?

GIRL. No, I don't think it was far from here.

WIFE. Very close, perhaps.

GIRL. Perhaps. (*Uneasy.*) But from up there it's not so easy to tell. If you're just passing on the viaduct.

The Sectarian opens the door to the poultry farm.

WIFE. Here we are.

GIRL (*claps her hands*). All those pretty birds!

SECTARIAN. Aren't they!

GIRL. Pheasants, guinea fowl!

WIFE. And doves.

GIRL. Yes, so many doves.

SECTARIAN. And many more on the roofs of the city, of course.

GIRL. How pretty they are! You'd never believe it, here in the midst of the warehouses and sawmills.

WIFE. Do you recognize it?

GIRL. What?

WIFE. The dove you saw.

GIRL. You think I'd recognize it?

SECTARIAN. We thought you might.

GIRL. I only saw it from a distance, from up on the viaduct—

WIFE (*quickly*). Was it this one?

GIRL. This one? No, it had darker wings.

WIFE. Or this?

GIRL. No, it had larger spurs.

WIFE. Then this one?

GIRL. It had a large helmet of feathers on its head.

SECTARIAN. Larger spurs, darker wings and a helmet on its head.

GIRL. But don't go to any trouble!

SECTARIAN. So it's not any of these?

GIRL. There are lots of others here.

WIFE. You wouldn't recognize it again?

GIRL. Do I have to recognize it? Isn't it enough that I saw it flying over the coal yards, that I saw it from a long way off? Why, why— (*Her voice metamorphoses into the cooing of a dove.*)

SECTARIAN. Enough questions!

WIFE. A fraction too many. (*Starts feeding the other birds.*)

SECTARIAN (*opens the cardboard box, takes the food out and shuts the dove inside*). In peace! The skies will welcome you!

Cries from the river below. The children have taken up their game again, but their cries are impossible to understand.

17

Vantage Point

The First Gnome emerges from one of the bottles piled in a heap by the garden wall.

SECOND GNOME. And? What's it like?

FIRST GNOME. Notes—pi—a— no—prac—tice.

SECOND GNOME (*giggles*). Throughout the garden?

FIRST GNOME. Throughout.

SECOND GNOME. And the light?

FIRST GNOME. Declining—also known as afternoon.

SECOND GNOME. Well learned! (*Laughs out loud.*)

FIRST GNOME. Quiet! Keep quiet in the bottle!

SECOND GNOME (*still laughing, but quietly*). Well heard!

FIRST GNOME. Well heard. (*Climbs a heap of last year's leaves, puts his hand on his breast, pathetic.*) Born from the dregs, listening through the open bottleneck, retained for— (*Stutters, breaking off.*)

SECOND GNOME (*delighted*). Retained for!

FIRST GNOME (*thoughtful*). For?

SECOND GNOME (*to the tune of a nursery rhyme*). Retained for, for, for! Retained for, for, for! Retained—

The First Gnome slides off the leaf pile.

FIRST GNOME. Keep asking questions!

SECOND GNOME. What's my nettle patch doing?

FIRST GNOME. Growing and flourishing. Budding as is its God-given right.

SECOND GNOME. And the old caterpillar?

FIRST GNOME. Asleep in the open air.

SECOND GNOME. The wine cellars and the dyeworks?

FIRST GNOME. Leaving the sky above them in peace!

SECOND GNOME (*restless*). The champagne cellars, too?

FIRST GNOME. Them too.

SECOND GNOME. And the police station?

FIRST GNOME. That too.

SECOND GNOME (*singing again*). Too, too, too—too, too, too, too—

FIRST GNOME. Blue.

SECOND GNOME. Blue too, blue too—too, too, too—

FIRST GNOME. Quiet!

SECOND GNOME. Quiet? (*Contemplative.*) How many questions have I got left?

FIRST GNOME. Seven.

SECOND GNOME. Too many!

FIRST GNOME. Three.

SECOND GNOME. Too few!

FIRST GNOME. Seven or three!

SECOND GNOME (*slyly*). If I were to ask you about the weather station, what would you say?

FIRST GNOME. I would say, the red train runs very fast past it in the distance.

SECOND GNOME. About the church wall and the library?

FIRST GNOME. The same.

SECOND GNOME. But about the villa owners?

FIRST GNOME. I would say, they are building pergolas and breeding deer.

SECOND GNOME. And about the vineyards?

FIRST GNOME. They are sloping.

SECOND GNOME. That's what you would say?

FIRST GNOME. Just that.

SECOND GNOME. Bor—ing!

FIRST GNOME (*correcting, patiently*). Af—ter—noon.

SECOND GNOME. But if I were to—

FIRST GNOME. If you ask me, you've already asked.

SECOND GNOME (*hops around furiously in the bottle, tries to break it*). Blown! Blasted! Bodged!

FIRST GNOME. Steady on.

SECOND GNOME (*after a while, once he's calmed down*). How many questions have I got left?

FIRST GNOME. Three.

SECOND GNOME. Seven or three?

FIRST GNOME. Three.

SECOND GNOME (*after much thought*). Is there a boy anywhere, sitting at his table?

FIRST GNOME. Yes.

SECOND GNOME. His father?

FIRST GNOME. Isn't at home.

SECOND GNOME. His mother?

FIRST GNOME. Nor her.

SECOND GNOME. His sister?

The First Gnome shakes his head, makes no further reply.

SECOND GNOME. His brother?

The First Gnome doesn't reply.

SECOND GNOME (*insistent*). His grandmother, his grandfather, his uncle, his aunt, all his cousins?

The First Gnome remains silent.

SECOND GNOME. Who walks to the telephone box and can't get a line, who to?

The First Gnome remains silent.

SECOND GNOME. Who lets the pigeons fly off?
Who lets the deer out?
Who colours the sky?

The First Gnome remains silent.

SECOND GNOME. Who refracts the rainbow above the vista of the city? (*Half-asleep.*) Is it him?

18

The New Song

*The Poet enters the front garden of the Eternal Rest Inn, opposite the ceme-
tery of a provincial city, looks around as if searching for something, walks
towards the inn.*

*The Landlady opens an upstairs window, watches him suspiciously as
he climbs the steps to the public bar, pauses a few moments there, then walks
back down. He is wearing a dark-blue frock coat, and a bow tie, but no hat.*

LANDLADY. Hello there!

POET (*shades his eyes with his hand, looks up*). Yes?

LANDLADY. Need something?

POET. A little rest.

LANDLADY. Rest?

POET. I would like to take a rest.

> *He sits at one of the tables, where there are still bottles from the night
> before, sparrows chirping loudly among them. The day is overcast. The
> street behind the dark-green woven-wood fence is quiet.*
>
> *The Landlady enters the garden and approaches the table, an
> older woman, her hair tied up roughly, only just risen judging by her
> appearance.*

LANDLADY. Take a rest?

POET. Yes.

LANDLADY. Nothing to drink, Sir?

POET (*shakes his head*). A room with a bed for the night.

LANDLADY. We don't rent rooms here.

POET. Would it not be possible?

LANDLADY. Just this once.

POET (*looks up at the Landlady*). I can't hold the town up any more.

LANDLADY. I think I recognize, Sir.

POET. That's possible.

LANDLADY. From a picture.

POET. Probably.

LANDLADY (*cautiously*). With a group of friends.

POET. Yes.

LANDLADY. My brother-in-law has it on the wall.

POET. Your brother-in-law, indeed?

LANDLADY. But there are other pictures of Sir? Might Sir be the poet?

POET. I am indeed.

LANDLADY. I recognize the coat.

POET. It would be very kind, Madam Landlady, if you could let me have the room for a night.

LANDLADY. As long as you're not fussy.

> *The Poet shakes his head. Brushes fallen leaves from the table with the back of his hand.*

LANDLADY. Doesn't Sir usually rest over there? (*Gestures with her chin towards the cemetery.*)

> *The Poet nods.*

LANDLADY. Beneath the obelisks next to the chapel of rest?

POET. I can't hold the town up any more.

LANDLADY. But I always imagine, when I'm awake at night, it would be good to be resting down there.

POET. That's what I thought when I was buried.

LANDLADY. That you'd get more rest there than at The Eternal Rest. (*Points to her inn, with its crumbling plaster.*)

POET (*shakes his head again*). It's a burden.

LANDLADY. I never knew Sir had to hold the town up.

POET. I only realized myself when I found I couldn't do it any longer.

LANDLADY. And is there no one to help, Sir? Lots of people have been buried over there in the last eighty years.

POET. Most of them just lie down under it.

LANDLADY. I'll help, Sir, when I come over!

POET. You're helping me already, Madam.

Suddenly the earth quivers. The bottles clatter against each other.

LANDLADY. Sir's room is in the attic.

POET. Anywhere is fine.

LANDLADY. I'll make up a fresh bed. (*Leaves.*)

While the Poet remains alone in the front garden, the earth calms down for a moment, but then the tremors return more forcefully.

LANDLADY (*from upstairs*). They used to warn us each time they were blasting over at the works. They never warn us any more.

POET. Don't put yourself to any trouble on my account, Madam.

LANDLADY (*returning to the garden*). But it's getting worse. The blasting is ruining my business.

POET. It doesn't bother me.

LANDLADY. The bed's made now. (*A large tremor. She stumbles, stands up again.*) It's never been this bad. I'll complain!

POET (*uneasy*). Might it be an earthquake?

LANDLADY. It's bound to be from the works. (*Stumbles again, looking intently at the Poet.*) Unless it's—

POET. It could be! (*Restless.*) Anyway if I can't have a room here at Eternal Rest, I'll look elsewhere.

LANDLADY (*in shock*). The Chapel of Rest opposite, the pink chapel of rest, it's got a crack! Running from the roof right to the ground and down into the earth.

POET. It's doing my soul a lot of good, that crack. (*Calmer.*) Do you know, Madam—just as you know about the dark nights—do you also know about the saint who turned in his grave when he noticed he'd been buried? They hadn't canonized him, although he was already beatified. But I, when I noticed I'd been buried, at the risk I might not be canonized, I rose up.

LANDLADY. Sir mustn't get himself worked up.

POET. Because I didn't want to be gazing with my own two eyes into the darkness the whole time.

LANDLADY (*as yet another tremor rocks the town, coming from the river*). The town is collapsing.

POET. I'm not holding it up any more. I'm glad I've flung the wilted wreaths aside.

LANDLADY. There was to have been a commemoration of Sir shortly. Then they would have been renewed—mid May!

POET. I've beat them to it.

LANDLADY. Afterwards there was to have been a meal here.

POET. I'm sorry if I've cost The Eternal Rest business.

LANDLADY. Doesn't Sir ever want to go back?

POET (*impatient*). For one night, for one night I want to sleep in a white bed, that's all.

LANDLADY. Does that mean for ever, when Sir says, 'for one night'? (*The Poet remains silent.*) I should go and look in the cellar, if Sir will excuse me, and check the barrels aren't leaking.

POET. Excused.

The Landlady leaves, as the tremors continue steadily and gently.

LANDLADY (*returning*). I think it's coming up from the river again, not from the works.

POET. Are the barrels still standing put?

LANDLADY. All still standing. (*Hesitant, slightly out of breath.*) But this isn't just about business and The Eternal Rest. It's about the town!

POET (*drums his fingers on the table*). About the town—the town!

LANDLADY. Sir must calm down first!

POET. That's easy for you to say, Madam!

LANDLADY (*calm*). Sir knows full well, that although something might be easier for one person to say than another, this never lasts long.

The Poet is about to erupt.

LANDLADY. When Sir calms down, Sir will be able to make the right decision.

POET. I have made it.

LANDLADY. Now the sun's coming out. Now even the cracks in the ground and in the Chapel of Rest look more friendly.

POET. They are the most friendly thing there is altogether. It's the undamaged Chapel of Rest, all the buildings, the sealed graves— they are what is unfriendly.

LANDLADY. If you have grandchildren living in town, and your sister marries someone in the new development, you learn to cope.

POET. Or on Sunday, that hour just after noon when the cocks behind the houses stop crowing and the sky closes over the earth on bright days like over a box of chicks. Without an air hole.

LANDLADY. For the likes of us—

POET (*calm again*). Once it was all very different—never mind during my lifetime, even shortly afterwards—

LANDLADY. The Eternal Rest goes back to that time. It had another name, but parts of the building, the foundations, are original. My grandfather, God rest his soul—

POET. That's not what I mean.

LANDLADY. The chapel of rest was painted differently, but otherwise—

POET (*irate*). Otherwise, otherwise! That's precisely the point. But you're determined to misunderstand me, Madam!

LANDLADY. Because I don't understand what can change from one day to the next for someone who is resting under the earth.

POET. The earth was different, Madam, the earth! Friable and yet firmer for my splayed fingers, solid and yet much looser on the chest, a dark map of the bright fields for all the poets down there. A better aid for the memory.

LANDLADY (*casts a glance at the crack in the earth*). It's quiet now, the earth.

POET. It's not to be trusted.

LANDLADY. Would Sir like to inspect his room now?

POET (*supports himself on the table as he stands up onerously*). Perhaps I should indeed lie down on the bed.

LANDLADY. Certainly. Sir is accustomed to lying down.

POET. I hadn't thought I'd have the urge again so soon.

LANDLADY. That's hard to believe.

POET. I'm remembering how even during my lifetime I didn't like climbing stairs. (*Brushing aside the Landlady who had tried to take his arm.*) What are you thinking of, Madam! God knows, I'm delighted if a memory comes to me at all. It's like in the very first time after I was buried. I could shout for joy!

They have reached the attic.

POET (*stretches out on the bed straight away*). Just what I needed!

LANDLADY (*opens the window*). A bit of fresh air for Sir.

POET. You are an angel, Madam.

LANDLADY. I can hear the fire brigades' sirens.

POET. My dear angel.

LANDLADY. Sir needs to sleep now!

POET. I'd like to sing. Air, air! No more earth on top of me! The town rhymes with me again, now I don't have to hold it up.

LANDLADY. The fire brigade still!

POET. In my time the first note was deeper, by a semitone—but that could be down to the horn.

LANDLADY. It's frightening me.

POET (*jubilant*). It's all coming back!

LANDLADY. Perhaps something has fallen in the town centre.

POET. That fine sky and the wind too.

LANDLADY. When my daughter-in-law goes shopping my grandchildren are on their own.

POET. That pink cloud over there!

LANDLADY (*absent*). That's from the works, where the riverside villages used to be, the primrose meadows.

POET. I'll put it in my song. As a pink dawn! It will be easy now. My fear has gone.

LANDLADY. If only I could go and check nothing has happened. If I could go into town for a look! But I can't, I'm on my own here.

POET. Go and check on your grandchildren, Madam. I'll be here at least that long. And If I hear the footsteps of a funeral party in the front garden, I'll go straight down and ask what I can get them. I'll find the wine, as long as the barrels remain intact. And I'll find the glasses. I'd rather play the landlord than the poet.

LANDLADY (*tentative*). If Sir is quite sure?

POET. I've always wanted to. My grandfather ran a tavern in one of the villages down on the river.

LANDLADY. Then I'll get organized so I'm back as soon as possible. I'll lock the doors so it doesn't make any difference, if Sir falls asleep—

POET. My God, when I remember the smell in the corridor! And the windows in the bar—from the street outside you could see through them to the river.

LANDLADY. Or if Sir begins to muse again, to start writing poetry, then it's no problem. Just if a large party arrives, please detain them long enough till I'm back.

The earth starts quivering again.

POET. Have no fear, Madam!

LANDLADY. I'll leave Sir a key. Then Sir can decide for himself if—

POET. I always wanted to be a landlord.

LANDLADY (*nervous*). The tremors have returned!

POET. The songs come more easily when you are waiting for guests than when you're lying down there with your arms crossed.

LANDLADY. I'm leaving now.

POET. Madam!

She is walking downstairs.

POET. Madam!

Her footsteps recede.

He stands up, sighing, bends out of the window.

POET. Madam!

LANDLADY (*wearing a black hat, heading out into town*). Yes?

POET. Could you just tell me where to find pen and paper?

LANDLADY. You can take some of the cash slips from the desk.

POET. The song, you see—

LANDLADY. You'll find a pencil there too.

POET. The second, the ultimate one—

LANDLADY (*hurrying, already in the distance*). Sir will find everything he needs.

POET. One that lives from the breath of the moment, not from memories, or even what we describe as such, memories of memories, the lump of earth on the bony palm, of which my poor souls says, 'From this were made the mountains in the first song, the river banks you wove in, the streets on which your sun played!' How soon they turn renegade, the poor souls, how soon they may turn to eulogize the earth. 'Hold it, hold it together! Admit that instead of reason, this is what lies within your skulls, and beneath your ribs instead of a heart. Admit that you forget, and that your song holds the old town up, as far as the invisible wall—and your bones the new town!' (*Raging.*) Accept, admit, for all eternity, admit it!

He has worked himself up into a fervour, leans out of the window and lets the wind blow through his hair.

POET (*calmer now*). Little has changed. The landlady is right. They have enlarged the cemetery, that's true. There are a few high towers on the right-hand edge which don't look like church towers, and above the Pfennigberg a bird is flying, larger than a vulture. But the clouds are mostly the same. Except the ones over the riverside villages—that looks like fire. (*Determined.*) I can swiftly tame you all. I can swiftly bring you into my song!

He opens the door and enters the dark stairway, humming to himself, feeling his way down the staircase, opens the door to the taproom.

POET. So it's here, here I am to regain my innocence, here I am to become truly immortal!

He pulls the drawer under the bar open, finds cash slips and a pencil.

POET. They'll be amazed, the people at the commemoration, with their fresh flowers (*Sits down at one of the tables at the back of the room.*) with their mid-May event. But I never imagined myself I'd be immortal already by the end of March, that it would happen so fast—faster than grass grows or trees blossom—that I'd find the air so light.

He puts pen to paper.

POET. (*A light tremor. The glasses on the shelf start clinking.*) Cheers!

He puts pen to paper again.

Footsteps on the gravel outside.

BOY. Is this The Eternal Rest, Dad?

FATHER. Yes, this is it.

BOY. Where my sister is lying?

FATHER. She's not far away.

BOY. It looks very quiet, The Eternal Rest.

FATHER. It'll look much better as soon as you've got a raspberry cordial in front of you. Hello, Landlady! (*To the Boy.*) You often have to wait here.

BOY. OK.

POET (*gets up and looks across the tables through the window into the garden*). A large party it isn't. (*Tiptoes, with the pencil in his hand, out from behind the table to the window, and quietly opens it ajar.*)

FATHER. Landlady!

POET (*to himself*). I don't really feel obliged.

FATHER. She's on her own, the woman—

POET. Just as a verse is forming in my head.

FATHER. She has a lot to do.

BOY. Is this the same Eternal Rest you often frequent, Dad?

FATHER. Twice a year, as a rule.

BOY. As a member of the Commemoration Committee?

FATHER. Yes.

BOY. For the famous man?

FATHER. For the poet, yes.

POET (*still at the window*). Definitely not now.

FATHER. He's buried near your sister, in the same row.

BOY. That will comfort her!

FATHER. We'll go to the grave once you've had your raspberry cordial.

BOY. And in May, Dad, when you give your speech—

FATHER (*proudly*). 'The Dead Poet'.

BOY. Then the wind will carry it to her!

FATHER. Yes.

POET. I'm not going out there now.

BOY. The earthquake was here, too, Dad!

FATHER. Yes.

BOY. It makes the earth so dry.

POET. I can't do it.

BOY. I'm thirsty, Dad!

FATHER (*calls out loudly*). Madam Landlady!

POET. If I go out now, I'll have to talk to them. I might have to identify myself. It could soon drive my song away.

FATHER. I'll look inside!

POET. My song! (*Slips back to his table.*)

FATHER. It's locked. (*Walks back to the table in the garden.*) There's no one inside.

POET (*back at his table*). I've got it now!

BOY (*to the Father, disappointed*). So that's why no one has answered.

POET (*returns to work with his pencil*). Now I'll write it.

FATHER (*to the Boy*). Then let's visit the grave first and come back later.

POET. It will vanquish thirst and vanquish hunger too! Vanquish uncertainty and also sadness. It will vanquish everything! (*Starts to write.*) It will be much more help to you!

BOY (*leaving—to the Father, patiently*). OK, later.

> *The next tremor splits the earth beneath the gravel and swallows the Boy and his father. The benches and tables are tipped aside and the bottles fall off. In the cellar the barrels start to leak. Cracks appear in the wall of the inn. The Poet leaps up and stumbles to the door.*
>
> *The Landlady enters the front garden from the road through a gap in the fence, which has been ripped out of the ground, stepping across potholes and over rocks, out of breath.*

LANDLADY. I never even made it into town.

POET. No?

LANDLADY. At the first tremor, the milder one, I turned back. And now—

POET (*bewildered*). Yes.

LANDLADY. Now, I'm here.

POET. I'm leaving again.

LANDLADY. Didn't Sir even lie down?

POET. No, I got straight up again. But now I'm going to lie down again.

He attempts to get to the exit through the planks and rocks.

LANDLADY. Give it a bit more thought, Sir!

POET. I'm going to lie down now.

LANDLADY (*sympathetic*). Take your time!

The Poet shakes his head.

LANDLADY (*more insistent*). Take your time, Sir. Perhaps it isn't because of you at all. Perhaps there's another reason for it altogether. Perhaps it's coming from the works!

POET. It's best if I lie back down under the earth so I can be certain. It's always been the most reliable way.

LANDLADY. It could easily be that something's exploded over there. Or that the earthquake has causes the likes of us have no idea about.

POET. Well, only the angels on the Day of Judgement know them. And even then it's unlikely they would divulge them.

LANDLADY. Sir could easily stay here a while. He could be a big help to me if he entertained the guests with his imagination while I serve drinks, or served drinks when I'm out.

POET. I'm not cut out to be a landlord, Madam.

LANDLADY. It would certainly benefit The Eternal Rest.

POET. I'll be more use if I lie back down. The Commemoration Committee—

LANDLADY. The Commemoration Committee could also meet to commemorate the living—

The Poet shakes his head again.

LANDLADY. It could meet more than twice a year!

POET. Even you don't believe that.

LANDLADY. If Sir were to give the occasional speech—

POET. Then I'd be stealing several people's thunder.

LANDLADY (*has taken her hat off, negotiating the remains of her fence*). Or if Sir just sat in the midst of everyone, in his dark coat—

POET. It would upset them, and not unreasonably, I can tell you now, Madam—

LANDLADY. And served the odd drink!

POET. I'm not serving drinks. As long as I can find one last cash slip behind the bar, and dust on the ground I can dip my finger in, I'll never stop writing words.

LANDLADY. Just a glass now and again, so they notice Sir sees himself as one of them!

POET. They'll notice that better if my bones are lying amongst theirs.

LANDLADY (*brushes her hair out of her face*). I'll be all on my own.

POET. Help me put it to the test, Madam, one test among so many! Think about your grandchildren, about all the houses, the whole town—as godforsaken as the thought is, and for that very reason. Let me go!

LANDLADY. Then let me wish Sir a good rest.

POET (*walking away*). And I wish The Eternal Rest all the best.

The Poet finds his way to the road, then disappears in the direction of the cemetery.

BOY (*has climbed out of the hole and helped his father out*). There's the landlady, Dad!

FATHER. Yes.

BOY. Can I have a raspberry cordial now?

FATHER. That is now the least of my worries!

LANDLADY (*calmly*). It's on its way.

19

Crossing the Mountain Pass

For Nelly Sachs

BOY. What are you doing today?

GIRL. I'm going to sort out my books. (*Laughs.*) But I'm giving the tablecloths in the linen cupboard the day off.

BOY. And then?

GIRL. Let's call the governess and ask her about this afternoon.

BOY. What about a drive?

GIRL. Do you think?

BOY. In the wind, with the garden chairs. Past all the closed shops.

GIRL. Or we could cross the mountains. With all the white animals! We've got so many white animals. If we include my fox and my rabbits, too?

BOY. But what about the pass?

GIRL. We can build that, easy. And then we can make the animals turn their heads in all directions all the time. And have a party at the top of the pass, in a hollow sheltered from the wind.

BOY. Cake and wine!

GIRL. Yes.

BOY. And the foxes and rabbits will never want to leave. I'll call her right now. (*Calls out.*) Miss Pelleas? Is there snow on the passes?

GIRL (*eagerly*). What does she say?

BOY. No snow.

GIRL. She always knows everything.

BOY. Only here and there, in the dips, where it won't upset the animals. Where we can't get past anyway.

GIRL. I wonder where she gets her information from. She's got someone.

BOY. You can ask her anything.

GIRL. A beggar with a gammy foot often comes to see her, a carpet salesman, may even be a gypsy.

BOY. A curtain salesman.

GIRL. That's someone else.

BOY. We'll ask her!

GIRL (*firmly*). Only if we really have to.

BOY. And till then?

GIRL. Till then best ask about the snow on the passes.

BOY. We know the answer to that.

GIRL. Or if she'd like to come and join us.

BOY. To cross the mountain pass with us!

GIRL. Ask her. Best ask right now!

BOY. Miss Pelleas!

GIRL. Louder!

BOY. Would you like to cross the pass with us?

GIRL. Tell her we'll take plenty of breaks!

BOY. We'll take plenty of breaks.

GIRL. And we'll have the sun from the garden on our heads, with the night-time wind from the dark rooms. We'll turn into elephants.

BOY. She knows that.

GIRL. And into china animals, pink and white, and into gold and granite animals, animals who come and visit, shimmering like mother of pearl, and animals who never come and visit. And we'll take flags and fog lights with us. The passes will be between the wicker chairs—

BOY. She knows all that.

GIRL. And the halos will shine down on us.

BOY. But what if she's waiting in for her friend?

GIRL. The saints' tales are hidden in the folds of the blanket along with the sea shores they'll need.

BOY. That won't entice her either.

GIRL. Colours like she'll never see for herself.

BOY. Poor thing.

GIRL. And sunsets, sinking stars, too.

BOY. But she won't want to.

GIRL. Why not?

BOY. I know her.

GIRL. But what if you tell her the cupboards are empty? That you can smell the wood, and smell five-hundred-year-old liquor in it?

BOY. Keep quiet! (*Puts his hand behind his ears.*)

GIRL. What's she saying?

BOY. What really entices her into our passes are the elephants. And the direction they're turning their necks. (*Listens out intently again, then repeats.*) There are chapels there with blue-black walls, she says.

GIRL (*eagerly*). We'll build them straight away!

BOY. No, wait! (*After a moment, disappointed.*) She's not saying any more. Nothing more for us. Just something about cigarettes for the postman, about dusters, and cacti which are meant to be flowering.

GIRL. But we know several things already.

BOY. Then get started!

GIRL. Cloudy outside, wind bringing snow. Pray to God it doesn't stop us building our passes, that we can find all our animals everywhere, that they don't slide off the blankets and shatter us.

BOY. And that perhaps an old elephant might turn his head to the walls of the room where the storms are sleeping, towards the blue-black shadows, the places we've kept for the chapel walls—

GIRL. Or just an ear.

BOY. An ear, just a little!

GIRL. That the darkness falls gently over us afterwards and that the snow in the dips lights us up till the last, but doesn't disturb any elephants.

BOY. Or us.

20

Nowhere Near Milan

SOLDIER (*sitting in a high-up window cavity in a burnt-out wall*). I can hear the colonel whispering behind me constantly. You too? Can't you hear it?

The audience say nothing.

SOLDIER (*climbs down two storeys*). It was here. (*Climbs back up a storey.*) No, here! (*Swings diagonally upwards, now sits in a cavity of what was once several windows.*) It wasn't here either.

The audience say nothing.

SOLDIER. What a grey sky, and thoroughly darkened by crows. Makes you worry it could go green again. (*Rather awkwardly.*) And send the eye to the horizon.

COLONEL (*appears in a window cavity on the other side of the wall*). It sent me to the horizon.

SOLDIER (*relieved*). There's someone there!

COLONEL (*losing his voice*). Way off beyond the Sea Saints' spires. It seemed green to me. (*Calmly.*) I was a lad then.

SOLDIER. I was never a lad.

COLONEL. Pity.

SOLDIER. I didn't fall near Milan either.

COLONEL. It's said to be a very fine city.

SOLDIER. So what? We're here now.

COLONEL (*sighing*). Yes. But it would be nice if we had more in common.

SOLDIER. I like it here.

Someone in the audience laughs.

SOLDIER. Who just laughed?

MAN (*with a shiny black hat, long coat and umbrella raises his hand*). Me.

SOLDIER (*taking little notice*). I see. (*Turns to the Colonel.*) Where were we?

COLONEL. Near Milan.

SOLDIER. That doesn't help much.

COLONEL. Not much, no. But it's warm up here.

SOLDIER. Warmer than you'd think.

MAN. We're freezing down here!

A PLUMP WOMAN (*also wearing black, stands up aggressively*). Yes, we're freezing!

Susanne appears in one of the lower window cavities in a white dress, remains as if in a picture frame without resting on anything.

SUSANNE. I can see the swans swimming round my father's house.

SOLDIER. What's she saying?

MAN. She can see the swans.

SOLDIER. You heard that!

SUSANNE. No doubt about it. All round my father's house. The floorboards make a racket when they swim over them.

The Soldier shakes his head.

SUSANNE (*dreamily*). They flap their wings wherever they can. That's where the words written along our roof beams came from.

SOLDIER. How do they go?

SUSANNE. I've forgotten. And when their wings are closed it's much heavier for the floorboards.

COLONEL (*sleepily*). Very interesting.

SUSANNE. The doors are all open wide ahead of them. (*Speaks louder, becoming effusive.*) The poplars have leant to give them wind, a storm in fact. The half-moon is rising. Oh all these staircases, these bannisters, these attic posts struts—

SOLDIER (*indifferent*). The elms, the roof-beam words—

SUSANNE. And the swans' words. We will share the world!

SOLDIER. Yes, half each.

SUSANNE. I can see the swans swimming round my father's house! (*Falls off the ledge, then vanishes.*)

SOLDIER. The swans.

SUSANNE (*reappears, her hair wild, her dress crumpled*). Oh yes, all round my father's house. They are carrying children's clothes on their backs, and as far as they can they are swimming around, in far, wide circles and through all the rooms, but they can't get under the bridge. Someone made them a promise, it was—

SOLDIER (*jaunty*). The south!

SUSANNE. It was the north.

SOLDIER. It won't keep its promise to you.

SUSANNE. No. Once they heard seven people facing the firing squad. Very close by.

SOLDIER. Who could blame them?

SUSANNE. Then then came into the house. My mother, in her white dress, gave them chunks of bread. It was a dark morning.

WOMAN. What's the point?

SUSANNE. That's why I'm seeing the swans.

SOLDIER. Oh I see, a white family.

MAN (*menacingly*). But what about you?

SOLDIER. I can still hear the colonel whispering behind me. It hasn't got any fainter.

COLONEL. (*Awoken from a short nap. Rejuvenated. Speaks contentedly.*) I can still remember the tales my father, God rest, told of the pirates who would breeze in from the north on warm days, straight over the flat fields to the church to boost the chorales.

SOLDIER. I hadn't been born then.

COLONEL. Undoubtedly not.

SOLDIER. But now the wind is getting up. Can you feel it?

MAN. It's howling through all the cracks.

SOLDIER. Isn't that the swans' wind, the wind which blows past the martyrs, the sickle wind crossing the fields, already topped with spume. What are they singing?

WOMAN (*suffocating*). What are they singing?

The martyrs' singing is heard.

COLONEL. I can't understand a word.

SOLDIER. No, but it's circling round the spires, round the spire of St Nicholas, of St Luke, around the Sea Saints' gates, the Three Kings' gates. If it's not coming from the north then it must be coming from the south. It's swirling and eddying. There are feathers all over the burnt-out city—

WOMAN. They're getting up our noses! I've got my pram with me, left from my eldest, but he is thirty now, and he was there. They tied him to an oak. He hung there for ages.

MAN. My eldest fell by a wall, like this! (*He demonstrates, hindered somewhat by his umbrella.*)

The martyrs' singing continues.

SUSANNE (*has woken up again; speaking stridently*). My dear swans, flap off upstairs, please. We need our dining table to dine on!

The audience starts grumbling.

SUSANNE. And the toys to play with, the willow to spread a cloth beneath, and plates, forks, knives—

SOLDIER. Little knives.

SUSANNE. And the bridge to throw stones off, yes!

The martyrs' singing gets louder.

SUSANNE. And my dear father is walking through his house again.

COLONEL. It's droning in my ears. I've made myself a little bed down there out of hay. (*Yawns.*) My children, my dear children—

SUSANNE. Bring us something from the zoo, Dad!

COLONEL. Oh, I've seen wolves running through the blinding snow, and not just once.

SUSANNE. A great dad!

The Colonel yawns.

SUSANNE (*pointing behind her*). Isn't it far too loud?

COLONEL. Yes, far too loud! Good night, my dear. Perhaps some time we might talk about Milan—about Milan, said to be very fine, or perhaps about Orléans, about Gotha—I have advised you of my hay bed and should be woken in advance—

SUSANNE (*pointing to the sky, excited*). The swans, the swans! Now they're flying off! (*Exhausted.*) I can see the swans leaving my father's house and all the spires are white with them. (*Falls from the window.*)

THE PLUMP WOMAN FROM THE AUDIENCE. Hey, you up there!

THE MAN WITH THE UMBRELLA. If you please!

WOMAN. We're waiting here in the rain.

SOLDIER (*calmly*). Now I can't hear anything. (*He remains standing in the window.*)

21

White Chrysanthemums

GENERAL (*an elderly man*). We should order coal.

GENERAL'S WIFE. I'm waiting for a woman who's bringing me flowers, white chrysanthemums for the graves. I've found a new florist's, not large, but reputable. They bring them into your house.

GENERAL. White chrysanthemums?

GENERAL'S WIFE. Yes, for the graves.

GENERAL. We've got it all covered—white chrysanthemums for the graves, pears for preserving, feathers for the pillows—they've got to be filled!

GENERAL'S WIFE. I have no idea what you're on about.

GENERAL. We've got them all coming here—apple ladies, pear ladies, flower ladies. Anything to distract us.

GENERAL'S WIFE. From what?

GENERAL. From the men who should be bringing coal. Every year we order our coal too late. We miss the early-bird discount and end up paying over the odds. If it was left to you we'd never order coal at all.

GENERAL'S WIFE. Only since the coal merchant's was taken over by that woman. I dislike her intensely.

GENERAL. The wife took it over?

GENERAL'S WIFE. Yes. The husband died.

GENERAL. I never knew that.

GENERAL'S WIFE. There's no other merchant near here.

GENERAL. I'll go there now. I don't know the wife or the husband that well but I do want to be warm when winter comes.

GENERAL'S WIFE. Calm down!

GENERAL. And I fancied a walk. I was just wondering where to head to anyway.

GENERAL'S WIFE. Also, today is Sunday.

GENERAL. Sunday? But what about your florist woman?

GENERAL'S WIFE. She delivers on Sundays. That's the thing.

GENERAL. Yes? Don't the taxis run on Sundays, too? Why don't you take one to the station and walk back? Why not? Why don't you! If the nurseries were open today I actually think you'd enrol ten little children who don't even exist. Just out of sympathy. But you won't order coal, whether it's because they don't open Sundays or just because you don't like the woman.

GENERAL'S WIFE. Because I don't like the woman. But I'll go there tomorrow.

GENERAL. Tomorrow we'll have to pay more. Tomorrow is the deadline. It's already winter, don't you understand?

The doorbell rings.

GENERAL'S WIFE (*excited*). That'll be the florist.

She goes out to open the door.

GENERAL. White chrysanthemums!

GENERAL'S WIFE (*comes back in with the Florist*). This is the nice, friendly florist I was telling you about, darling. And whether you choose to believe it or not, now you can see she does come on Sundays! She comes into your house, all the way up to the fourth floor.

GENERAL. The sheer quantity!

FLORIST. White chrysanthemums.

GENERAL. I expected nothing else.

GENERAL'S WIFE (*to the Florist*). This is perfect, dear. What lovely flowers you've brought! They will make the graves look really respectable again.

GENERAL. Our graves would look perfectly respectable with or without chrysanthemums. Even with just green grass growing over them, even just bare earth—

GENERAL'S WIFE. But this way they look much more respectable.

GENERAL (*furious*). That's enough!

FLORIST. Can I put the flowers down here? (*Points to a dark corner of the room.*)

GENERAL'S WIFE. Of course, my dear. (*Enchanted.*) The way they glow!

FLORIST. Yes, they are beautiful. But you shouldn't let them get too warm.

GENERAL. Oh they won't get too warm.

WIFE. We'll take care of that.

FLORIST. Otherwise we can't guarantee they'll still look fresh by the flower deadline.

GENERAL. What deadline?

GENERAL'S WIFE (*beaming*). The flower deadline.

GENERAL. Saint Valentine's?

GENERAL'S WIFE. No, try and understand, darling—it's the deadline for an early-bird discount on flowers.

GENERAL. That does surprise me.

GENERAL'S WIFE. Indeed.

GENERAL. It coincides with the deadline for coal.

GENERAL'S WIFE. There isn't one every year, only every— (*Looks inquiringly at the Florist.*)

FLORIST. Every seventy or eighty years.

GENERAL'S WIFE. That's why not everyone knows about it.

GENERAL. No, not people who die at five.

GENERAL'S WIFE. And so I thought—

GENERAL (*sharply*). What?

GENERAL'S WIFE. We should take advantage of it. We should put flowers on all the graves, while there's still time—our parents' and grandparents' graves, all our close relatives', all our— (*Pauses for breath.*)

GENERAL. That's what you thought?

GENERAL'S WIFE. Yes, and not only that. (*Smiles mischievously.*) I thought about possibly putting some on our own graves!

GENERAL. Oh yes?

GENERAL'S WIFE. Yes, darling.

GENERAL. That would require us to be lying in them.

GENERAL'S WIFE. Not straight away. We would have to be there within— (*Looks at the Florist inquiringly.*)

FLORIST. Three weeks.

GENERAL'S WIFE. Exactly. Within three weeks.

FLORIST. But the earlier the better.

GENERAL. Well, that makes sense.

GENERAL'S WIFE. Of course. What do you reckon? Do you think in fourteen days' time we could get everything—

GENERAL. Everything?

GENERAL'S WIFE. Well, of course—

GENERAL. Why not be ready in eight days? Or even better three? Or ideally today, by lunchtime, before all the churchgoers come home?

GENERAL'S WIFE. Darling!

FLORIST (*modestly*). The gentleman and lady opposite have ordered Chinese foliage plants. And the people further down have ordered tulips for the church.

GENERAL'S WIFE. Tulips!

GENERAL. Not a bad idea either.

GENERAL'S WIFE. But white chrysanthemums are better. (*To the Florist, anxiously.*) Aren't they?

FLORIST. They are rather the thing.

GENERAL'S WIFE (*delighted*). You see?

FLORIST. They still shine out once everything else has faded.

GENERAL'S WIFE. Is the freshness guaranteed?

FLORIST. Yes, but the flowers need to be taken up there soon, so they don't dry out.

GENERAL'S WIFE. We'll set straight off!

FLORIST. Ideally, three days before the funeral.

GENERAL. At that point we'll be busy dying.

FLORIST. In that case, half a day earlier.

GENERAL'S WIFE. How do other people handle it?

FLORIST. Most of the ladies and gentlemen take a taxi straight up there. Some of them take the bus then change onto the tram, but very few of them—

GENERAL'S WIFE. Darling, let's go right now! It's Sunday and I'm a bit worried the few taxis in the neighbourhood will all be taken.

GENERAL (*calmly*). Right now?

GENERAL'S WIFE. Yes, now. We can eat a late lunch, then sort our things out—

GENERAL. And die around 6 p.m.?

GENERAL'S WIFE. That's what I was thinking.

GENERAL. Have I understood correctly, that because of the early-bird discount on flowers our whole street plans to give up the ghost?

FLORIST. Several ladies and gentleman have made the decision, but by no means everyone.

GENERAL. That surprises me.

GENERAL'S WIFE. Me too.

FLORIST. The most attractive graves receive an award.

GENERAL. I was aware of that.

GENERAL'S WIFE. So which families have already decided?

FLORIST. I can't disclose their names.

WIFE. You see? It's best we decide right now! If we hesitate any longer they'll all beat us to it.

GENERAL. Indeed. They would then beat us to it.

GENERAL'S WIFE (*eagerly*). It's up to us, Alfred.

GENERAL. One more question.

FLORIST. A question?

GENERAL. It's about the clouds over the cemetery.

FLORIST (*has paled*). The clouds over the cemetery?

GENERAL. I mean on the day the flower discount ends, the day after our death. (*Without letting her get a word in.*) Will it be mignonette-coloured, pink or pale-green?

FLORIST. Mignonette-coloured, pink or pale-green?

GENERAL (*sharply*). I'm asking what the sky will be like. Damp, slate grey, like the paving stones at dusk or the pigeons' feathers as they fly up briefly from the church square in the morning?

FLORIST. Like the paving stones at dusk or the pigeons' feathers?

GENERAL (*walks towards her*). I'm asking. And I'll tell you. You know. It will be red, the sky, lacerated and seething!

FLORIST. I don't know a thing. I can't say anything. I—

GENERAL. Get out of here!

> *The flowers and the florist vanish. There are two bright, reddish patches of sunlight on the parquet floor.*

GENERAL'S WIFE (*to the General*). Where are you going?

GENERAL. To order our coal. After that I'll go and feed the pigeons on the church square.

22

Chrigina

MRS WRAY. St Peter? (*Waits.*) No answer. It reeks of glass and dilap-
idation here. I need to hang the sign up properly.

She shuffles back downstairs.

MRS WARY (*pausing again*). St Peter? Nothing! No knocker on the
door either. You have to use your fists.

We hear her hammering and then coming back.

MRS WRAY. Where has he got to this time? Riding the elephants'
trunks, along the canal. The school will fold. Our lovely little
school, where Chrigina was so happy. Pity.

ST PETER. Mrs Wray!

MRS WRAY. Yes?

ST PETER. I'm here. (*Mrs Wray says nothing.*) I hadn't been anywhere.
I was intending to go—

MRS WARY (*snaps*). When weren't you?

ST PETER. To the harbour, to visit a sanatorium for sailors from small
ships. It's called the Lilliput Hospital. I've been meaning to get
there for ages.

MRS WRAY. I know you.

ST PETER. You know me very well. Who could know better than you how fed up I am of the paths through the parks, how my rusty beard upsets me—yet I leave it. And the rest.

MRS WRAY. Yes.

ST PETER (*ingratiating, tormented by his weakness*). I see you've attached a cord to the latch.

MRS WRAY. So it's easier to open.

ST PETER. What is?

MRS WRAY. The door, dear fellow.

CHRIGINA'S FATHER (*from outside*). Chrigina!

MRS WRAY. Listen to that, again!

ST PETER. Only once this time though.

MRS WRAY. God knows where the little one is.

ST PETER. Yes, it's easy to slip under the radar. And children like that have hiding places you'd never guess—between the paving stones, or behind racks of piano stools, organ pipes, at the Royal Academy. Chrigina says, 'Listen, I'll change into a chicken, or into something else. I'll wait till my daddy stops searching.' At least she might—or she might say nothing.

MRS WRAY. Stop it!

ST PETER (*singing to himself*). I am a poor old soldier,
I saw the king of rats
And watched him come and go
From my nice green pillow.

MRS WRAY. Stop it!

ST PETER. OK.

MRS WRAY. You have no boundaries.

ST PETER (*concerned*). No luminosity. A dim light against the stones. It billows into the rooms and then peters out.

MRS WRAY. I'd pull myself together again.

ST PETER (*preoccupied*). You would? Yes, of course.

MRS WRAY. If I had the urge.

ST PETER. Grey or brown, ragged. Bedded down under the world. And always with the urge.

MRS WARY (*sharply*). Rather useful for opening schools.

ST PETER (*determined, like someone saying 'I'm leaving'*). I'll stay then.

MRS WRAY. I worry about your decisions. I'd rather place each and every one of them out of your reach, they're so vulnerable.

ST PETER. Penned in.

MRS WRAY. With a little green-tinged light to grow up in; better colours, a memorial for horses, Leonidas.

ST PETER. Nymphs?

MRS WRAY. Just a few.

ST PETER. Adieu, my dear!

MRS WRAY. If only we could all go! Away from Chrigina's father and his tired cries. To some place where all that means little.

ST PETER. To a beautiful place.

MRS WRAY. Yes. And away from this stairwell. It really is draughty here.

ST PETER. We could both go.

MRS WRAY. Neither of us can. Actually I think he just wanted to go fetch bread.

ST PETER. Uttering cries like that?

MRS WRAY. Same as ever. He'll enrol her again. One of these days he'll come back and say, 'I'd like to place my daughter in your care!' and I'll reply, 'Why certainly, Herr . . . Herr . . .' Oh, what's his name?

St Peter laughs.

MRS WRAY. He'll doff his battered top hat for me.

St Peter breaks into laughter again, starts coughing.

MRS WRAY. And I'll lead her upstairs again and teach her needlework again with the window open, the various patterns and stitches— (*Sighs.*) It does the world of good.

ST PETER (*calmed, impassive*). He's called Herr Taube.

MRS WARY (*relieved*). That's right—Chrigina Taube.

ST PETER. A vulnerable girl.

MRS WRAY. Easily toughened up.

ST PETER. And with a little push, returned to the world.

MRS WRAY. With a very quick shove.

ST PETER. Your shoves, Mrs Wray!

MRS WRAY. Famous over the years. Rated by various authorities, cited in dining rooms.

ST PETER. A boy cracked his last nut against them with his heel.

MRS WARY (*outraged*). You—

ST PETER. I found it unseemly.

MRS WRAY. But nothing worse.

ST PETER. I've gone along with your rules long enough, Mrs Wray. We've shared many worries, architectural proportions, subjects like dam construction, model ship construction—

MRS WARY (*dismissively*). Curriculums, lesson plans! (*Mimicking him.*) Who's sweeping the bottom staircase today, my dear fellow?

ST PETER (*exhausted*). I've been constantly reborn in your niches.

MRS WRAY. Among candelabras, quickly rustled up. And that's as far as it went. You never bothered once. Do you recall our argument about the confetti?

ST PETER. Yes.

MRS WRAY. And much more besides

ST PETER. All of it, all the time.

MRS WRAY. Lucky no one entrusts their daughters to you any more. In your four walls up there.

ST PETER. There aren't four. The first is just painted, and the third—

MRS WRAY. But lots of places to hide, oh— (*Laughs ecstatically.*) plenty!

CHRIGINA'S FATHER (*from outside*). Chrigina!

ST PETER. The wind is really blowing. In cahoots with you.

CHRIGINA'S FATHER (*rests his arms on the sole window in the hall*). Has anyone seen my daughter?

MRS WARY (*taking no notice of him*). When I think of everything which could happen! (*Throws her hand up in front of her eyes; suddenly starts crying.*) Flagstones, wicks going crazy—

ST PETER (*clears his throat*). Mrs Wray!

MRS WRAY. And eternal happiness! A blurred vehicle, off down the street!

CHRIGINA'S FATHER. All information gratefully received, no obligation. I've been down to the customs boats already.

MRS WRAY. You needn't have done that.

ST PETER. Nothing on their lists?

CHRIGINA'S FATHER. The lists were soaked. From below, you know?

MRS WARY (*in another outburst*). Your daughter mastered cross-stitch with us!

ST PETER. With you alone, Mrs Wray.

MRS WRAY. She had some structure. She was secure. In the afternoon she would help herself to bread and apples from the basket.

ST PETER. What else should she have done?

CHRIGINA'S FATHER. I've beaten myself up about that long enough.

ST PETER. There's nothing else she can do, old chap.

CHRIGINA'S FATHER. My sole consolation, a sorry drawing of the Tibetan hills. In the foreground a carter bends over his barrel, in the background the lessons are noted in red chalk.

ST PETER (*lively*). Damn right!

MRS WRAY. So will that be all?

CHRIGINA'S FATHER. Not for me it won't.

MRS WRAY. Again and again you manage to lead us up the garden path. At the end of the day you only have yourself to blame—

CHRIGINA'S FATHER (*urgently*). Yes, yes! That's what I want!

MRS WARY (*furious*). That's what he wants. That's what this is about. That's his sole concern! We should never have returned her to you.

ST PETER. We never should.

MRS WRAY. How true.

ST PETER. I'd just like to draw your attention to the moss in the courtyards at the mission schools. They are often paved with rectangular stones, convex, and between them grows moss. No dust, no nutshells—

MRS WRAY. Which reminds me! (*She starts sweeping the dust away.*)

ST PETER. But no nuts either.

CHRIGINA'S FATHER. Sometimes she used to want pears. 'Daddy, can I have pears!' The things she wanted.

MRS WRAY. Nothing surprising there then.

ST PETER. If I were you I would—

CHRIGINA'S FATHER (*eagerly*). Yes?

ST PETER. Request a formal investigation.

CHRIGINA'S FATHER. A formal investigation?

He makes a cautious exit while St Peter reflects further.

ST PETER. Back to the ships, the white horses, the Arabian horses. There are many more there. The sparky steps and that whole rough neighbourhood down there— (*Looks up, notices the empty window.*) but it's no fault of our establishment, and you can rest assured we've done everything we can—

Sweeps his hair back and rushes out of the building.

ST PETER (*in the distance*). Herr Taube, Herr Taube!

MRS WARY (*mimicking him*). Chrigina and Herr Taube, Herr Taube *und* Chrigina! One thing they're good at— (*Plonks the broom down audibly*) bringing our dear old school into disrepute. And nothing else.

Nothing more is seen or heard from Mrs Wray.

23

Alms

The Almoner is at a desk in a dark room, writing. Raises her head as she hears the door open.

ALMONER. There you are, Johanna!

Johanna, young, a little shadowy, leans in the doorway.

JOHANNA. Yes.

ALMONER. Did it go all right?

JOHANNA. Very well.

ALMONER *(slightly impatient)*. Sit down, child. I'll be finished in a minute.

Johanna quickly sits down on a chair near the door.

ALMONER. Terrible weather, isn't it?

JOHANNA. It's still raining. (*Changes abruptly.*) I've given away all the shoes.

ALMONER. Properly? With best wishes each time, and my greetings?

JOHANNA. Yes.

The Almoner continues writing

JOHANNA. Where there was no one in, I left them with the neighbours. Some of them were in the middle of packing, so it was good timing.

ALMONER. Excellent, excellent.

JOHANNA. One boy was at the swimming baths so I gave the shoes to his mother. And two of the children were home alone.

ALMONER. Were they pleased?

JOHANNA. Yes. They said they were just the shoes they needed for their game. It's called the tower game. Do you know it?

ALMONER. No.

JOHANNA. 'Hansel, dear Hansel,' the girl was singing.

ALMONER (*laughs*). That'll be Hansel and Gretel you met.

JOHANNA. The boy was called Joseph. The hallway was so full of packages it was hard to get through, but they weren't theirs.

ALMONER. I know that house. (*Carries on writing.*) And did you tell them all it's possible the shoes might not fit? Too large, or too small, or whatever?

JOHANNA. I passed everything on. And then I crossed the bridge—

ALMONER (*preoccupied*). Yes?

JOHANNA. It was windy there, stormy actually. At the church, the blonde girl gave me a big hug. I've forgotten her name.

ALMONER. Gertrud.

JOHANNA. Yes, that's it, with the plaits. She seemed grateful, from the way she acted. I gave her some shoes too.

ALMONER. She lives right next door.

JOHANNA. And some to the fishmonger for her grandchildren.

ALMONER. Hopefully to the right one, like I told you.

JOHANNA. It was quiet over there, not many coffee houses. But the storm almost ripped the packages out of my hands and blew the brown paper away.

ALMONER (*raises her head*). It'll soon rip the roof off over our heads, but it won't do us any harm, will it?

JOHANNA. No.

ALMONER. Won't stop us doing what we're called to do, will it? (*Continues to write.*) I'll give you some more shoes later.

JOHANNA (*hesitant*). I think everyone has enough shoes now. They're not grateful

ALMONER. No?

JOHANNA. If they were filled it might be a different matter. But they aren't filled.

ALMONER. We can't do everything.

JOHANNA (*quickly*). They just pretend to be grateful. But they don't know what to do with them and how they're going to pack them.

ALMONER (*dismissively*). Most of them are light, felt slippers or summer sandals, opanci for hot weather and open shoes for in-between times. All of them easy to pack. They can be popped in on top. Obviously, if someone really doesn't—

JOHANNA. There is such a thing as too many shoes. It can actually make people's stomachs turn, when they see all the shoes.

ALMONER. If they've got it too good.

JOHANNA (*ignoring her*). You could, for instance, find yourself craving bishop's mitres, white and gold, piled up in the stairways. If you bump into them they sway, but they don't fall down. Mountains of bishop's mitres!

ALMONER. That's not seriously your heart's desire.

Johanna stays silent.

ALMONER. And instead of being pleased that someone still bothers at all—

JOHANNA. They aren't so easily pleased.

ALMONER (*sighs*). There you have it.

JOHANNA (*while she carries on writing*). Should I leave again?

ALMONER. I don't know Johanna. (*Hearing the chair move.*) No, stay put! Give me a bit of peace for a moment and let me finish writing! Then we can carry on talking about the shoes.

JOHANNA. Or you might fancy ice stalls, stalls put up on the river I mean. Stalls with fires on the bare ice, which can be shunted along.

ALMONER. Enough of your cravings!

JOHANNA (*sternly*). I'm not talking about myself.

ALMONER. Not yourself?

JOHANNA. No, I don't mean me. I would crave very different things.

ALMONER. I wouldn't be talking like that at a time like this.

JOHANNA. Or if I were you.

ALMONER. What are you saying?

JOHANNA. If I were me.

ALMONER (*looks up intently*). Perhaps you should come back later, Johanna.

JOHANNA. Not much later.

ALMONER. So you don't distract me from my writing.

JOHANNA (*intrigued*). Are you doing the maths for the bishop's mitres?

ALMONER. Who said anything about bishop's mitres? Bishop's mitres and ice stalls are a long way from my thoughts.

JOHANNA. But it is maths you're doing.

ALMONER. I have more important matters to consider—hospital visits, a bunch of lilac for old Frau X, rescuing a child.

JOHANNA. And that.

ALMONER. Because there's a large number of children at risk.

JOHANNA. And you can't help all of them.

ALMONER. But here and there you can. You go and find out more, you lend them books. People have no idea the power that resides in books.

JOHANNA. That's true. I once read about ice jams and salt-mine minions. That helped me for ages.

ALMONER. You have no clue. There are people living in cubbyholes in the cellar or between the rafters in attics. It's freezing there in winter and boiling in summer.

JOHANNA. Compared to that I've got it good.

ALMONER. If only you could see it.

JOHANNA. I can come in and out here, and you say to me, 'Sit down, child!'

The Almoner laughs.

JOHANNA. But some things still pass me by.

ALMONER. Indeed.

JOHANNA (*comes closer*). What is this maths for?

ALMONER (*reluctant*). Who says it's maths?

JOHANNA. It looks like numbers.

ALMONER (*exasperated*). Please go and get some fresh air, child! Go and talk to the porter—

JOHANNA. He's gone shopping, with the big bag. I saw him just now.

ALMONER. Or to someone else. See if you can find the cat and bring her in.

JOHANNA (*dejected*). OK.

ALMONER. Count the posts on the bannisters in the hall for all I care, just don't disturb me here.

JOHANNA. I'll go in a minute. But can't you tell me what you're writing?

ALMONER. I'm not obliged to.

JOHANNA. I mean whether they're numbers or something else?

ALMONER (*stands up and starts stamping her feet*). Go away!

JOHANNA. Or just names which look like numbers. You get that too. If you write five or six names in a short row (*Laughs nervously.*) it looks as if you were adding them up.

ALMONER (*calmer now*). Just go!

24

The Untired Sleepers

A Scene from a Play

The funeral parlour of a crematorium seen from the left-hand side. On the raised platform, knocked up out of planks, is a wonky stand for the coffin, alongside it two candles and a few meagre flowers. No side walls, the roof supported by two iron poles. Along the wall behind the bier is a black pleated curtain, a long way to the side of it, towards the auditorium, is a small door. Steps lead down from the platform on both sides and at the front. Out in the open, outside the funeral parlour, are three rows of wooden benches, rough and without back-rests. When the curtain is raised no one can be seen. At the front, on the end of the third row of benches is a black cape. After a few moments the Vicar enters the funeral parlour through the small door, cautiously, wearing a worn-out cassock.

PRIEST (*wiping the sweat from his forehead, calls into the empty room*). No one here yet?

After a few moments, without another person being seen, a shiny, wooden coffin is pushed through an opening in the curtains.

PRIEST. Mr Schwarz!

The electric candles light up.

PRIEST (*louder and somewhat helpless*). Mr Schwarz! (*Checks the time.*)

From the cemetery which surrounds the funeral parlour come two women. They are in a hurry, running finally, and sit down swiftly at one end of the first row of benches. When they see the Priest they leap up, just as swiftly, and switch to the middle of the second row. After taking a quick look around, the taller, stronger-looking of the two takes a dark, wide shawl which she has been carrying over her arm, and spreads it over both of their heads and shoulders. They move closer together. The Priest moves a little closer to the edge of the platform, which is not secured by railings.

PRIEST (*calls down*). The Bounty cremation?

The Women look at each other, but don't answer.

PRIEST. Are you here for the Bounty cremation?

THE OLDER WOMAN. Bounty, that's us.

PRIEST. Emily Bounty.

THE OLDER WOMAN. She would be in there.

THE YOUNGER WOMAN (*nervously*). Can we be sure of that?

THE OLDER WOMAN (*assertively*). Could we please check?

PRIEST. No.

THE OLDER WOMAN. Our sister has already been denied a stab through the heart. Tim Candy had one, but when it came to our sister the coroner said, 'If I say someone is dead, they are dead.' (*After a moment.*) I'd like to see him try that with me, but I won't be using him. I'll use Dr Peebles.

THE YOUNGER WOMAN. It's perfectly possible it's all true, Lavinia.

LAVINIA (*angry*). Oh anything's possible. There's always a faint possibility!

PRIEST (*loudly*). Mr Schwarz!

LAVINIA. I saw him earlier on his bicycle. Near the heroes' graves.

MARIE. He's very fast. (*Animated.*) Here he is!

A man in a grey work jacket rides calmly along the far side of the stage, vanishes behind the funeral parlour and after a moment steps out onto the platform.

SCHWARZ. I was here earlier.

PRIEST. Me too. Are we expecting any other mourners?

SCHWARZ. That's always hard to say. (*To the two women.*) The vicar wishes to know if anyone else is expected.

MARIE. Is he talking to us?

SCHWARZ (*louder, while straightening up a candle*). Is anyone else coming?

MARIE (*timidly, to Lavinia*). Do you think Dad—

LAVINIA. It doesn't look like it, does it?

MARIE. But Dad?

LAVINIA (*to Schwarz*). As far as we're concerned you're welcome to start.

MARIE. Our father—

PRIEST. Your esteemed father—

LAVINIA. It was always as if our esteemed father wasn't there, even before we came along.

PRIEST (*turned half towards the Women, half towards Schwarz*). Should I begin then?

SCHWARZ. Yes.

Marie starts sobbing quietly.

PRIEST (*hesitantly*). Then I'll begin.

He steps down three of the wooden steps, takes his cape from the bench and climbs back up. He opens and closes the door he came through and walks towards the coffin.

Marie sobs louder.

LAVINIA (*to Marie*). He looks a little like us. (*To the Priest.*) Fire away! My sister is crying already.

PRIEST (*helpless*). Your esteemed sister—

LAVINIA. This esteemed sister, the one next to me. My other esteemed sister isn't crying any more, the one next to you.

PRIEST. Now then.

SCHWARZ (*uninvited, but speaking clearly, one hand over his eyes to shield him from the sun*). No one else is coming now.

PRIEST. Ladies and gentlemen!

LAVINIA (*to Marie, still sobbing softly*). Did you hear that Marie?

PRIEST (*louder*). Ladies and gentlemen! (*Quietly to Schwarz.*) Relationship to the deceased?

SCHWARZ. Sisters.

PRIEST. Dear esteemed loved ones of the dearly departed—

LAVINIA (*to Marie*). He's an donkey.

MARIE (*who has stopped crying*). I like him.

PRIEST. Dear ladies and gentlemen of the dearly departed, who, at the age of thirty-seven—

LAVINIA (*loudly*) Thirty-seven is correct.

PRIEST (*bewildered*). At the blessed age of thirty-seven—

LAVINIA (*to Marie*). There's something wrong with this. It'll come to me.

PRIEST. Of thirty-seven years— (*Stutters.*)

SCHWARZ. The two ladies must let the vicar speak.

MARIE (*imploringly*). See, Lavinia?

SCHWARZ (*more insistent, but calm*). Because your esteemed sister is not the only one today.

LAVINIA. Poor Emily, I thought—

SCHWARZ. (*firmly*) She is not the only one.

LAVINIA. Arguments like this—

MARIE (*in desperation*). Lavinia!

LAVINIA. Are the kind of thing you always have to steel yourself for. Reverend—

PRIEST (*wipes the sweat from his forehead, helpless*). Ashes to ashes, dust to dust.

MARIE (*accusingly to Lavinia*). See?

PRIEST (*moving on quickly*). Ladies and gentlemen, with these words let us bid farewell to the dearly departed. The dearly departed—

MARIE (*nervously to Lavinia*). Don't say another word!

PRIEST. She demonstrated, that no one need die in an overcrowded psychiatric ward, that we can face the end without stress or anxiety, that we can sink in to the arms of the almighty without fear—

Lavinia is seized by a coughing fit which she quickly suppresses.

PRIEST. Not tied to a bed with leather straps, but free, standing tall and actually at home. On her last day, she got up out of bed at her customary hour. Despite her poor state she put the kettle on the stove and opened all the windows.

LAVINIA (*whispering*). He's crazy.

PRIEST. But not to get fresh air herself. She stripped her bed, pulled the blankets back, flung the pillows aside—

LAVINIA. And turned straight to the sewing basket.

PRIEST. Exactly. As it later transpired, after her sewing she planned to write a joint letter to her friends and relatives abroad, but didn't manage it in time.

LAVINIA (*her arm even more protectively around the sobbing Marie*). Thank God.

PRIEST. Her death was exemplary, a needle and thread in her hands—

LAVINIA. And a knee-length sock, so ragged as to be unrecognizable, belonging to one of her distant cousins.

PRIEST (*determined not to be interrupted again*). Her head bowed, it was swift, showing consideration for the rest of the family, for her father and sisters, for the whole procedure, when she could equally have engaged in a long, anxious battle with death.

LAVINIA. Bravo. Or Brava. Not sure how you say it.

MARIE (*whispering*). Lavinia!

PRIEST. She was found.

LAVINIA. That was the height of consideration.

MARIE (*sobbing*). Emily!

PRIEST. She was laid to rest. Just as she was.

LAVINIA. She was washed too.

PRIEST. Her face peaceful. She was easy to lift onto the bier, but will not easily be condemned when the time comes. (*Wipes the sweat from his forehead again.*)

LAVINIA. We don't doubt it.

PRIEST. Thirty-seven years. Imagine what that means. It means first becoming eight years old, nine years, ten. It means first celebrating your eighteenth, your nineteenth, twentieth. It means first reaching twenty-seven years, twenty-eight, twenty-nine, and it means—

Marie rips the scarf from her head, lets out a brief, high-pitched wail then collapses down again, pulls the scarf back over her head, assisted by her sister.

LAVINIA (*numb*). Have some consideration for us.

A gaunt, white-haired man enters the stage, with a shotgun under his arm, climbs onto the platform from the right using the steps. He examines everything in detail and stares down at the two black figures.

MAN (*breathing out, after some consideration*). Thank God we're all white and British.

MARIE (*shocked*). Father!

FATHER (*sternly*). White and British.

LAVINIA. I saw this coming.

SCHWARZ. Are you part of the funeral congregation, Sir?

FATHER. I'm part of the whole thing.

PRIEST (*respectfully, with a gentle bow*). The father.

LAVINIA. And his dammed daughters. Suddenly he's with us.

FATHER. First let's fire a shot at the sun.

PRIEST (*respectfully*). My deepest sympathies.

FATHER (*raises his shotgun without a second thought, shoots*). Good morning, dear sun. we wouldn't want to start without you even today.

LAVINIA. We would. And without you, Dad.

FATHER. Shut your mouth, Lavinia. You should have been a son.

LAVINIA. Shouldn't everybody?

PRIEST. Again, my deepest sympathies.

FATHER (*walks affably towards the priest*). Thank you, Vicar, my Emily really was a good girl.

SCHWARZ (*standing behind him to one side*). My heartfelt condolences.

FATHER (*bows in his direction*). Thank you, too. And let me say it again, thank God we're all white and British. It does at least give one the right grounding in impossible situations such as this.

SCHWARZ. If Sir might now step down so the service can be concluded.

FATHER (*slips out with his shotgun through the side door.*) Thank you, Sir. But I prefer to visit the heroes' graves. I'll be there if anyone needs me.

SCHWARZ. Did you fire a shot just now from over there?

FATHER. Me? Yes. Are we not allowed to salute the sun from that particular spot?

SCHWARZ. Not too often. It can get out of hand.

FATHER (*shaking his head, walking away*). Get out of hand!

LAVINIA. He won't understand that.

SCHWARZ. A lot of people choose not to.

LAVINIA. Indeed.

PRIEST. Shall we proceed to the more comforting part of the service?
He sits down at a harmonium positioned in the background and strikes a chord, starts to sing the hymn 'Zion's daughter, O rejoice!' before he is interrupted.

A young man enters from the right, staggering.

LAVINIA. Andrew!

ANDREW. Here you are.

MARIE (*timidly*). This is our brother. Come here, Andrew!

ANDREW (*making his way through the narrow rows of benches towards his sisters*). Was that Dad scouring the sky over this haven of peace for birds he's forbidden to shoot?

MARIE (*softly*). Dad.

ANDREW (*hugs his youngest sister*). Little Marie! (*Over her head, to Lavinia.*) Has it begun already?

LAVINIA. It began ages ago. The vicar was just about to start the more comforting part.

ANDREW. What's that? (*Lays his head in Marie's lap.*) I'm so tired.

LAVINIA. Keep still, will you!

MARIE (*strokes his head*). Stay there.

ANDREW (*tries to sit up*). I'd like to know what that is. (*Drops back down.*)

PRIEST (*who had got up, now sits back at the harmonium and starts to sing again after the introductory chord*). Zion's daughter, O rejoice! (*Stops, then carries on playing when Marie joins in.*)

MARIE (*softly*). Shout aloud, Jerusalem! Lo, thy King doth come to thee—

PRIEST (*as Marie breaks off singing in tears*). Yea, he comes the Prince of Peace!.

ANDREW (*while the Priest plays the rest of the hymn and Marie, now with her head on Andrew's knees, is convulsed by sobbing*). Is this the more comforting part?

MARIE (*disconsolate*). I think so.

The Priest leaves the platform, climbs down the side stairs, walks along the first row of wooden benches and attempts to shake the sisters' hands over it.

PRIEST. My deepest sympathies, sympathies, deepest sympathies!

He wipes his face with his handkerchief.

ANDREW. They keeping you busy, Reverend?

PRIEST. It's all right. So! (*Leaves in the direction Andrew had entered.*)

ANDREW. So it's all right. Where is Emily then? (*The coffin has now been taken into the building's interior.*)

Marie doesn't get up, starts crying quietly again.

LAVINIA. Do you have to keep asking silly questions, Andrew?

ANDREW. Have you dealt with the paperwork already?

LAVINIA. Yes.

ANDREW. Or was it Dad?

LAVINIA. We did it.

ANDREW. I wasn't free at the time you see.

LAVINIA. Nor was Dad.

SCHWARZ (*who has placed two bouquets and a wreath on the edge of the platform*). I need to know what's happening with the flowers.

ANDREW. Whatever normally happens.

MARIE. Would you like to keep them?

Schwarz shakes his head.

MARIE (*quietly to Lavinia*). Should we perhaps give the man a little something—

ANDREW. Naturally.

He starts looking in his pockets, finds nothing. Meanwhile Lavinia stands up, looks in her handbag, takes out a note and slides out from the benches.

SCHWARZ. You must excuse me, Ladies, Sir, but I'm always being offered these flowers. And yet ever since I was a child I've hated cut flowers. And there are just too many of them.

LAVINIA (*has now reached the platform and Schwarz; she hands him the note*). Hopefully not too many of these.

SCHWARZ. My sincere gratitude.

LAVINIA (*hanging the wreath over her arm and taking the bouquets*). We'll take these with us then.

ANDREW (*rushes over, Marie following him*). Little sister, little sister, don't strain yourself! (*Relieves Lavinia of the wreath, hangs it round his neck, then takes the bouquets too.*)

SCHWARZ (*while closing the black curtain behind the platform, vanishing behind it*). Then once more my deepest sympathies, ladies and gentlemen.

ANDREW. Rather a lot.

LAVINIA. Take the wreath off your neck, Andrew. And give me and Marie the flowers. It looks like you're making fun of the whole thing.

ANDREW (*calmly*). I just wanted to make myself sad. I'm not really feeling anything.

He gives each of the sisters a bouquet but leaves the wreath hanging round his neck.

From a little further away, we hear several shots in quick succession.

LAVINIA. Sounds like Dad is still close by.

MARIE. Further off than just now.

ANDREW. Our sweet Marie. (*Puts his hand on her shoulder.*) Always ready to take a little of the embarrassment out of embarrassing situations. (*Lets his hand drop. To Lavinia.*) Was he not here?

LAVINIA. He was here.

ANDREW. And how did he behave?

LAVINIA. He walked straight onto the platform and fired his gun.

ANDREW. In honour of our Emily?

LAVINIA (*curtly*). In honour of the sun.

ANDREW. That sounds like him.

MARIE. She's leaving already.

ANDREW (*points with his head to the faint smoke emerging to the left of the platform*). Emily is banishing it, good girl.

LAVINIA (*sternly*). Andrew!

ANDREW. We should leave too.

MARIE. Perhaps we should steer clear of the heroes' graves.

ANDREW. Gladly. I know a side-exit.

He takes his hands out of his pockets, links arms with his sisters and starts walking with them in the direction he came from.

LAVINIA. Could you not take that wreath off your neck before we leave the cemetery?

ANDREW. I can do a few things. But not many.

They walk faster, and exit. For a moment it remains quiet. The Father returns from the other direction.

FATHER. My two girls not here any more? Marie? Lavinia? (*He notices the black curtain, raises his head and observes the thinning smoke.*)

There's been a lot of changes here. Let's just say, you take seventy more steps, fire two or three more shots, and the world takes on a completely new appearance. Bravo Baldwin! (*Pats himself on the shoulder.*) But the smoke will have sent them packing. It can blur your vision even close up. (*He takes a few steps, but then stop still and looks over at the smoke.*)

Bravo Emily, I nearly forgot you. You always did things properly and you seem to be doing things pretty well now, too, as far as I can see. You were always an unassuming girl, withdrew as soon as someone so much as came over to talk. And now, too, heavens! But have no fear, it's only your old father, looking over your shoulder for a minute before he goes back to the others and reignites the pointless conversations. 'My dear, I must say in the few days I haven't had the pleasure, your arthritis has improved markedly. Already read the new one from old Swift? Only half? Half is always the best.' (*Interrupts himself, pauses for a moment.*) It looks like the smoke is turning too. You really are an astounding girl, Emily. And I can see you will remain one.

He walks away, the shotgun over his shoulder, in the direction the others exited.

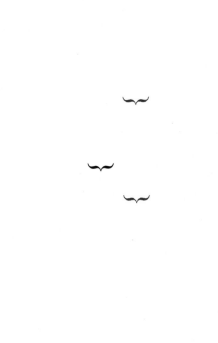

Editorial Note

A majority of these dialogues were first published in *zu keiner Stunde* (Frankfurt am Main: Fischer, 1957) and were written between 1954 and 1956. In 1980, it was updated to include: 'Nowhere Near Milan' and 'White Chrysanthemums', both written in 1959; 'Chrigina', written in 1960; and 'Alms' (n.d.). 'Through the Mountain Pass' (1961) and 'The Untired Sleepers' (1980) were added to the 1991 edition, the final edition, on which this translation is based. Most were never performed publicly, except for *French Embassy*, broadcast as a radio drama on Bayerischer Rundfunk in 1960.